Help for the Small-Church Pastor

Help
for the
Small-Church
Pastor

Unlocking the Potential
of Your Congregation

STEVE R. BIERLY

ZondervanPublishingHouse
Grand Rapids, Michigan

A Division of HarperCollinsPublishers

Help for the Small-Church Pastor
Copyright © 1995 by Steve R. Bierly

Requests for information should be addressed to:
Zondervan Publishing House
Grand Rapids, Michigan 49530

Library of Congress Cataloging-in-Publication Data

Bierly, Steve R.
    Help for the small-church pastor : unlocking the potential of your congregation / Steve R. Bierly.
        p. cm.
    Includes bibliographical references.
    ISBN: 0-310-49951-8 (softcover)
    1. Small churches. 2. Pastoral theology. I. Title.
BV637.8.B54 1995
253—dc20   95-06143
                                                        CIP

Edited by Lisa Eary
Interior design by Joe Vriend

Printed in the United States of America

96 97 98 99 00 / ❖ DH / 10 9 8 7 6 5 4 3

Acknowledgments and Dedication

Thanks to friends and colleagues who through the years have helped me shape my philosophy of ministry: Paul Caley, Rodney Collins, David Currence, Mel Emurian, Crystal Etzel, Robert Evans, James Foster, Perry Fuller, Chuck Hesselink, Craig and Jan Hoffman, Dick Brian Klaver, Doug LaBudde, Jr., Al E. LaValley, Candace Lawrence, Gerald C. Matatics, Jack Peters, John Sheldon, Randall Stone, Don Troost, John VanderTuin, Jack Van Dyk, and Carlton Walker.

Thanks to Nancy Clark, former Reformed Church in America Associate for Small Membership Churches, for urging me to get my ideas published.

Thanks to Stan Gundry, Jim Ruark, and Rachel Boers of Zondervan Publishing House for their support and guidance.

Thanks to my parents for raising me in a Christian home and demonstrating God's unconditional love.

Thanks to my children, James and Abigail, for lighting up my life and for being excited that Daddy was working on a book.

Thanks and all my love to my wife, Deborah—editor, typist, critic, fan, encourager, listener, supporter, lover, and friend—to whom this book is dedicated.

91086

Contents

Note:

The stories in this book are true, or are composites of real situations, unless otherwise stated. Only names and minor details have been changed to protect the innocent—and the guilty, for that matter.

Introduction:
The Good Race or the Great Waste?

I almost demanded my money back! I had come to this two-day seminar to learn how I could lead my small congregation to numerical growth. Yet the speakers all admitted, with sheepish grins, that their ideas wouldn't work in small, established, traditional congregations. In fact, the speakers urged those of us who served in small churches to resign and go plant new congregations based on the principles outlined at the seminar. When it came to small churches, "let the dead bury their own dead" was the speakers' motto. If I wanted to be on "the cutting edge" of what God is doing today, I had to kiss the small church good-bye.

I suppose I shouldn't have been surprised at the speakers' attitudes. After all, they were only verbalizing what many people believe—that God's relationship with the small congregation is like a young man's relationship with his ninety-two-year-old great-grandfather who is in a coma in the hospital. The young man is sorry to see his great-grandfather in this condition. He feels a sense of love and obligation toward his great-grandfather, mostly based on things that happened in the past. He visits his great-grandfather once a week, but it seems like a waste of time. Great-granddad doesn't respond to anything or anyone anyway. What kind of a life is that? There is a part of the young man that just wishes the doctors and nurses would turn off the life-support machines and let great-grandfather die already.

In the thinking of many, the small church is like the great-grandfather. It won't respond to any outside stimuli, and God must be wishing that it would die already. Then he could get on with his life and spend his time hanging out in the Crystal Cathedral, Willow Creek Community Church, and Coral Ridge.

Often the powers that be in denominations and even within small churches themselves don't really expect much to happen in these churches. Lyle E. Schaller points out that in the United Methodist Church, for example, small churches are likely to "have a series of very short pastorates, usually four years or less"; "be perceived by many members as a post-seminary apprenticeship for young pastors on their way up the conference ladder of appointments"; and "not be expected by denominational leaders to grow in size."[1]

Many pastors don't expect much to happen in small churches either. A young pastor confessed to me, "When I came to this church three years ago, I threw myself into the work. I tried to start new Bible study groups, researched outreach programs, and set about to determine how the congregation could best minister to the community. However, I soon discovered that the people here weren't interested in any of that stuff. Basically, they want me to preside at business meetings, preach a sermon during the worship service, teach an adult Sunday school class, marry, and bury—and that's it. So that's all I do. I've given up trying to move them forward." When I asked if he was happy, the pastor sighed, "No, but at least I have a job and can support my family."

I saw a chilling preview of what this pastor might be like at the end of his career when an older pastor told me, "I feel as though my entire life has been a waste. If I had it to do all over again, I would never choose to spend my productive years ministering in my small congregation. Get out and move on while you can, Steve. It's too late for me now. Pastors nearing retirement tend to be consigned back into small churches."

Yet I also know a minister who felt differently when he retired from a lifetime of pastoring small congregations. He looked back on his years of service with gratitude, particularly the eighteen years with his last church. This pastor blessed the

Lord that he had made him worthy to shepherd the dear people the pastor was leaving behind. He marveled that the church had been changed through his ministry. The lay leadership had caught his vision and pledged themselves to continue the programs he had started. Although they were deeply sorry to see their pastor go, they believed that, through his ministry, God had prepared them for great things ahead.

Before this pastor's experience is written off as "there are some good congregations out there and he just happened to find one," I need to explain that the church was not perfect by any means. They still wrestled with the kinds of problems that cause pastors to bail out of small churches: inadequate facilities; power struggles; meeting financial obligations (how to pay off a mortgage and pay a pastor at the same time); clashes between newcomers and longtime members, traditionalists and progressives, older and younger generations; lack of volunteers to staff the Sunday school and other programs; and "Just whose responsibility is it to turn up the sanctuary heat before choir practice, anyway?"

All of these problems left their mark on the pastor. He wasn't a Pollyanna nor a Mr. Spock who could convince himself, "There is no pain. There is no pain." He had spent long days and sleepless nights burdened with the cares of the ministry. However, through it all he developed a very biblical, positive attitude toward small-church ministry. He viewed the congregation not as enemies or stubborn people who stood in the way of what needed to be done but as beloved and valuable brothers and sisters for whom Christ died (1 Corinthians 12:4–13; Ephesians 5:25–30; 1 Thessalonians 2:8, 11–12). He always looked for the good that he was sure would come out of even the most intense struggles because he was sure God was at work, building and refining the church (Matthew 16:18; Romans 8:28–39; Philippians 1:3–6; 4:4–8; 1 Peter 1:3–7). It was this positive attitude that enabled him to stay on the job so many years and was the key reason the congregation followed his lead.

Unfortunately, as my seminar speakers illustrate, a positive attitude isn't always easy to find. Small-church leaders can be prone to discouragement, frustration, and despair. This is in part because we fight with our sinful, fallen natures. Also in many cases the training we've received; books and articles we have read; and our high-speed, instant-gratification, "go for the gusto" world has given us unrealistic expectations for small-church ministry. The small church is often found to be wanting when viewed through the eyes of the church growth movement or proponents of the latest fad sweeping evangelicalism.

But how does God view the small church? Like my happy, retired pastor friend, I believe God looks at the small church and sees much good there. He calls leaders to discover and focus on that good and to find ways to strengthen and increase it. This approach is the key to having a successful, fulfilling, and faithful ministry in a small church. This book explains why this approach is necessary for small churches and how it can be applied.

PART ONE

Why the Best-Laid Plans Go Awry

CHAPTER ONE

But I Followed the Instructions!

"Ministry is not a rational enterprise. In fact, it may seem totally irrational at times."
—Roy M. Oswald[1]

Pastor Young's congregation was stalled out at forty adult members. Pastor Young was firmly convinced that evangelism was the mission Christ had given the church, but he just couldn't seem to get his people excited about it. Then Pastor Young attended a retreat sponsored and paid for by the denomination. The theme was "Reaching Your World with the Gospel." Pastor Young soaked up everything the speakers had to say. By the end of the week, just as the retreat leaders had promised, he had an "Action Plan for Outreach" ready to present to his board.

While at the conference, Pastor Young had met Matt Ryan, another man ministering in a small church. Pastors Young and Ryan were about the same age and shared a passion for evangelism. All week long they psyched each other up. Matt's last words to Pastor Young at the airport were, "We know what needs to be done. Now we have to do it. No more excuses. Fight the good fight, bro. I'll be praying for you."

At the first board meeting after he returned, Pastor Young presented his plan. And a masterful presentation it was. First, he went into the scriptural basis for soul winning. He quoted denominational experts on the necessity of growth. He told how churches that were similar to his congregation had been able to add new members. Finally, he presented the steps his church needed to take in order to grow.

The board listened with a polite interest during the whole presentation. Then one member broke their silence. "Pastor, I just don't see what's so wrong with our church being the size it is."

"Yeah," another spoke up. "After all, God must love small churches. He made so many of them." The board members laughed heartily.

A third offered, "Weren't there house churches in the Bible, Pastor? They couldn't have been very big. To me the important thing is not the size of a church but whether or not it faithfully proclaims the Word of God."

Before Pastor Young could counter that the Word of God gives the Great Commission to the church, the first board member spoke up again, "You know what I believe your trouble is, Pastor? I believe that you have a real problem with being content where God has placed you. It's a common problem with pastors, but it's one you're going to have to deal with, or you'll never be happy in the ministry."

The others began chiming in with "solutions" to the pastor's "problem."

"You should pray and read the Bible more."

"If we're not keeping you busy enough, use your extra time to bone up on theology."

"Maybe the real trouble here is your wife. Doesn't she like our church?" And on it went.

Pastor Young left that night with his head spinning. What happened? The next day he got on the phone with some friends and colleagues. They all counseled him to hang in there but to back away from the growth issue for a time. They thought that the congregation would eventually be ready to hear what Young had to say. It just wasn't God's timing yet. Maybe God wanted the congregation to work on relationships or to weed out sin before he would grant growth. And

Pastor Young was just the kind of man God could and would use to accomplish these things.

About a year later Pastor Young began to feel that the time was right to bring up the subject with the board again. This time he gave a very streamlined presentation and a truncated action plan. The board, however, waved the whole thing aside with one member's comment, "Church growth ideas don't work in our geographic area." It was still "not yet God's time." The pastor retreated to his office to work on a new growth strategy that he hoped the board would accept down the road.

It was then that Pastor Young heard about Matt Ryan. He had been forced to leave his church—literally. Matt had a "breakdown" in the pulpit and had begun ranting and raving against the congregation. Two of the elders bodily removed him from the sanctuary. "Matt, old buddy," Pastor Young sighed to himself, "I know just how you feel."

A year and a half later, Young did know exactly how it felt to be forced out of a church. At a board meeting that had been called specifically to discuss his latest outreach proposal (which he had distributed copies of in advance), the board set aside the scheduled business to ask for his resignation. The reason Pastor Young was given? "You never do anything to move this congregation ahead!"

The women's organization was in serious trouble. None of the younger women wanted to join and the older ladies were, to put it bluntly, dying off. Soon Cherry Valley Baptist Church wouldn't have a women's group. Cathy Gordon, a young mother of three, grew tired of hearing the older women complain and of reading announcements in the church newsletter like this: "Wednesday, June 2, 7:00 P.M., Cherry Valley Ladies Fellowship—Aren't there some more of you out there who'd like to join us?" Cathy knew why the group had no takers. The format of the ladies fellowship hadn't changed much in twenty years, and neither had the attendees. The meetings opened with a brief one- or two-minute "devotional"—often a poem or story from a women's magazine—followed by what seemed like endless "discussions" (arguments actually) about whether or not to spend the group's funds and/or how to earn more. Finally, the evening was capped off with refreshments and maudlin news about everyone in town who was dying. Even if a young woman were to go to the trouble of hiring a sitter and/or missing a night with her spouse to attend, the meeting was hardly incentive enough to generate the type of ongoing commitment from her that the group desired.

Cathy felt that there must be a better way to run a women's group. She got the number of the denomination's office of women's ministries from the pastor and placed a call. What she learned was very encouraging. The denomination could provide just the help the women needed to keep their organization going. The denomination published Bible study guides for fellowship groups to use. The office also passed along many suggestions for mission and community service projects. Cathy believed that a Bible study/service group would appeal to women of all ages. So she decided to go to the next ladies fellowship meeting and let them know what she had discovered.

Rather than viewing the denomination as their salvation however, the ladies fellowship seemed upset by what the office had to offer.

One woman asked, "Cathy, are you saying there won't be a ladies group anymore?"

"No, just that it would be different."

"Well," an influential matron huffed, "I don't think I would come to such a group. If I want a Bible study, I'll go to the adult Sunday school class."

"I don't think that changing things will make anybody else attend," another spoke up. "The younger generation won't commit to anything."

At that point, Cathy decided not to mention that the denomination's regional office had a consultant who could help the fellowship reorganize. Instead she determined she would remain just as "uncommitted" as her peers.

———

Messiah Church was ready to purchase land for its first building. The small group had been meeting in a rented high school auditorium, but now it seemed as if the church was going to get a place of their own. Pastor Brudam had worked long and hard with the committee checking out various sites, contacting realtors, and determining what the church could manage financially. A meeting was set up with a realtor to go through final negotiations.

Pastor Brudam didn't believe he should be the church's representative at the meeting because, as he explained it, "I've never bought property in my life. I've always lived in rentals and parsonages. Plenty of you are more experienced than I am in these matters. Besides, according to our denomination's book of church order and our congregation's own bylaws, I'm not even a member of this congregation. I'm a member of the presbytery. I can't legally sign any papers because in the eyes of the state I'm not an appointed representative of this church." This made sense to the committee, and they decided to send to the meeting one committee member and one board member who could sign for the church. They also agreed that the pastor's presence was not necessary.

The day of the meeting, Pastor Brudam remained in his office by the phone to wait for the results. Although he was anxious to hear what happened, he was confident that he had done the right thing by not going to the meeting. Besides the reasons he had given the committee, he had recently read an article by one of his seminary professors who stated that pastors burn out because they try to do too much. Pastors should concentrate on prayer and teaching and leave the "running of the church" to their congregations.

Suddenly, his phone rang. It was the board member. The deal had fallen through. The pastor's heart sank but went even lower when the board member gave the "reason."

"It's because you didn't care enough about this church to attend the meeting," the board member screamed.

"What do you mean? How did my not attending affect the outcome of the deal?"

"Don't change the subject. The issue is that you don't give a rip about what happens to this congregation and your actions show it!"

"But Phil," Pastor Brudam said, "you know why I didn't think it was right for me to go to the meeting. You agreed with my reasons. What in the world happened at the meeting?"

"All I know," Phil growled, "is that the board is going to hear about your attitude." And he hung up.

Sure enough, at the next board meeting, Phil raised the issue of the pastor's supposed lack of concern and gave example after example to support his case. Pastor Brudam began to answer Phil by showing that in every case, as with the realtor's meeting, he had logical and right reasons for doing what he did. Suddenly other board members jumped in, cutting the pastor off. They also felt he didn't care enough. Pastor Brudam was shocked. Where was all this coming from?

———

Linda West was excited. Although she and her husband had only been members of the small church for a year, she had been asked to serve on the board. The reason given was, "We need some fresh blood. We need new ideas. Input from younger people is valuable to us."

Oh, did Linda have ideas and input to give! Linda was a reader. When she became a Christian, she devoured not only books on personal discipleship but also books on what the local church could and should be and how it needed to restructure itself to survive in the future.

At first, she eagerly attended the board meetings to share her vision for the congregation. But her ideas always seemed to mutate during the board's discussions. For example her plan to start home fellowship groups (from the book *You Can Have a Caring and Sharing Church* by a metachurch expert) somehow became, "Pastor, why don't you take a few more prayer requests from the congregation during the service Sunday mornings?" Her desire for a freer worship atmosphere (like the one she read about in *Sing to the Lord with the Newest Songs*) led to the board declaring that one Sunday evening service a quarter would be a hymn sing. When she expressed her strong conviction that each congregation should be doing something for the poor and needy (a conviction she gained as she read *They Can't Eat Sermons: How to Really, for Sure, this Time No Kidding, Impact Your Neighborhood for Christ*), Linda was reminded by the board that the women of the church already sent flowers to anyone in the congregation who experienced a death in the family.

It soon became crystal clear to Linda that the congregation had no intention of doing much of anything beyond what they were already doing. Disgusted, she began skipping the board meetings. One Sunday she suggested to her husband, "I hear the Lord's doing some great things over at Grace Community Church. Let's check it out this morning. Just for a change." Not too long after that the Wests made the change permanent.

Pastor Johnson went to the board meeting confident that action would be taken against the trouble-making elder. The man had circulated a letter among the church members criticizing the new choir director and her choice of music. Pastor Johnson opened the meeting by reading Matthew 18:15–17 and other passages which outlined the correct way to handle disagreements and conflicts within the church. The pastor assured the board that he had brought up the matter with the elder but was ignored. He then shared that the choir director was deeply hurt and ready to leave the church because of the elder's action. The pastor told the board about the phone calls he had received concerning the letter, and he urged the board to move quickly to restore unity in the church.

Pastor Johnson even knew what action needed to be taken. The photocopies of the denomination's book of church order he had distributed to the board members clearly spelled out what to do when an elder was in sin. In addition, the pastor handed out copies of an article, "When a Leader Stumbles," from the denomination's magazine. Pastor Johnson then called on the elder to publicly repent or face the discipline that was outlined.

The room was silent. One of the other elders cleared his throat and said, "Well, Pastor, we just don't think that what Ralph did was so bad. Let's just forget it and move on. What's the next order of business?"

Pastor Johnson couldn't believe his ears! Hadn't the board been listening to him? The sad answer was that they had indeed heard him, but they weren't interested in taking any action against good old Ralph. Case closed.

Is it any wonder that leaders in small churches become disgusted with their congregations? After all, when the leaders attempt to follow the guidance of the experts—professors, authors, seminar speakers, denominational executives, and pastors of successful churches—their efforts are often thwarted by their congregations. Small churches ignore, dismiss, or openly rebel against the good advice experts provide. Therefore, these churches must be filled with unrepentant, hard-hearted, close-minded, sinful, stubborn people. Right?

While it's true that something is certainly wrong somewhere, is it necessarily the people in the small church? If the experts' advice doesn't work, maybe something is wrong with the advice.

At the very least, the experts' advice could be wrongly applied. A missionary going from the United States to India wouldn't take along books on how to reach baby boomers. Indians aren't concerned about sermons entitled "Where Is God When You Have to Change Jobs," or churches that offer low-impact Christian aerobics, or worship services that include musical selections from the Rolling Stones, Garth Brooks, Amy Grant, and DeGarmo and Key. A missionary would be foolish to become angry with people because none of these things interested them. Methods that work perfectly well in suburban America would be totally inappropriate in the Indian culture.

Many of the experts operate in a culture that is very different from that of the small church. Lyle Schaller says that moving from large churches to small ones "requires developing a new model for ministry."[2] Roy Oswald calls going from a large church to a small church "a cross-cultural barrier as tough as any foreign mission field." He also maintains that "the difference between seminary religion and parish religion is greater than the difference between denominations."[3] So when the experts are from academic circles and/or large churches, their advice is perfectly fine for leaders ministering within those worlds, but totally inappropriate in the world of the small church.

Recognizing this will help leaders go a long way toward

developing the positive attitude that is essential to survive and thrive in the small church. Leaders are being foolish when they become angry with small congregations who fail to be motivated by ideas that are alien to their culture.[4] The small church cannot be a seminary or a megachurch. There is no sense in trying to make it into one. The wasted effort will only bring frustration and heartache. The small church is simply a different animal, and its main differences will be explored in Chapters 2, 3, and 4.

CHAPTER TWO

Out of the Ivory Palaces

"In seminary I learned to discuss infra- and supralapsarianism, and yet in thirty years of ministry, I've never had to use that knowledge. But I've encountered lots of unreasonably angry people, and I was never even warned they'd be out there."
—an unnamed pastor quoted by Marshall Shelley[1]

In the academic and business worlds from which most ecclesiastical experts come[2] (not to mention most pastors and lay leaders),[3] the key to success is hard work.

"For the next thirty days," the professor of my January session course informed us, "you will eat, drink, sleep, and breathe Hebrew. At the end of the month, you'll be ready for any Old Testament exegesis course this seminary has to offer."

And he was right. In seminary, the path to success is clear: study, study, and then study some more. If one puts in the time and effort, one is assured of the Master of Divinity degree. Even if one's term or exegesis paper takes a position that is contrary to the professor's, as long as the paper is well thought out, logical, and neat and makes its points by appealing to the proper authorities, church history, and the Bible, it will receive a good grade. Hard work and clear thinking are rewarded.

Even when seminary students move out of the library to the field for some "hands on" experience, they know that if a problem comes up, it can be taken back and shared with their reflection group. A student writes up the problem as a case study, presents the paper, and then listens as colleagues pool their brains and resources to come up with the solution that will advance the church of Jesus Christ, minister effectively to those involved, and save face (maybe even a job). Once again the message comes through that all problems can be handled if one reflects long enough and utilizes the proper resources.

Having been indoctrinated in the "Hard Work Guarantees Results" school of thinking, the seminary graduate accepts his or her first call confident that a well-stocked personal library, subscriptions to quality pastoral journals, a phone network of friends who can dispense good advice, and time set aside to use all the above will lead to church growth, a spiritually-mature congregation, and offers from larger churches. The conferences and seminars the pastor attends reinforce this mindset. They teach that everything rises and falls on leadership. If you are a strong, knowledgeable, hard-working leader, the sky is the limit for your church (not to mention your career).

It all sounds good. It even sounds noble. "I accept full responsibility for the state of my congregation. A group can only go as high as its leader will take it. I'm going to work my hardest to take my church higher and higher. No excuses. If my congregation goes nowhere, it will only be because I have been sluffing off on the job." But there's one little problem with believing that effort, study, and good resources will bring success—it doesn't always work in the real world.

———

Pastor Findley was thrilled to see the Carson family attending worship services, even though he knew that they had some doctrinal differences with the church. Greg and Pat were young, attractive, and enthusiastic, exactly the kind of people his staid congregation needed. So what if their views on baptism and the end times didn't match his? These were surely minor issues at best. Besides, once the Carsons were exposed to his solid teaching and biblical preaching, they would come around. In fact, they eagerly accepted the books on baptism and end times that Pastor Findley loaned them. And hadn't Pat told him at the door last Sunday that he was giving her and Greg a lot to think about?

Time passed and the Carsons seemed to be happy, actively participating in the life of the congregation. Imagine Pastor Findley's shock when Greg called him on the phone to say that he and Pat were leaving. "We just don't believe the same way that you do," Greg explained. The pastor asked Greg for an opportunity to meet with him and Pat.

And meet they did. Over the course of the next three weeks, they met three times for two to three hours at a sitting. Between meetings, Pastor Findley dug out his seminary notes on baptism. He reviewed the scriptural basis for his eschatological viewpoint. He asked several pastoral colleagues to pray about the situation. He engaged in mock debates with several trusted elders in order to be prepared for any point the Carsons might raise. And he always went to his appointments armed with pages of research crammed into his Bible. But the meetings went nowhere.

Finally, at the end of what turned out to be the last meeting, Greg sighed and said, "I don't know the Bible as well as you do, Pastor, but I know what I believe."

"But ... but, you've just admitted that I have a better understanding of Scripture than you do. Why then can't you accept that my positions have merit?" Pastor Findley sputtered.

Pat chimed in, "It's true we can't answer your arguments, but we have to go by what we feel deep inside. We have to leave the church."

And they did.

———

"I think we're losing our children," the junior high Sunday school teacher sighed. "They act bored, like it's a big burden for them to be in class."

The fifth and sixth grade teacher spoke up. "My bunch, too!"

"Maybe we could look into trying some new material," the superintendent suggested. "There are some really imaginative curriculums on the market now. I'd be glad to look into what's available and report back at our next meeting."

Everyone agreed that this would be a good idea and was exactly what they needed to bring new life to the Sunday school department.

So for the next two months, the superintendent threw herself into what was, for her, the enjoyable task of researching what the different publishing companies had available. She met with the pastor to determine which programs would be compatible with the church's theology. She haunted the local Christian bookstore, browsing through its stock and ordering sample kits of the lines that appealed to her. She prepared a chart that clearly showed the strengths and weaknesses of the various curricula. She prepared a report that she would deliver to the group. Finally, before the meeting she set up a display of materials from what she considered to be the top three publishers.

After she made her presentation, she invited the teachers to come up to the front tables to look for themselves.

Nobody moved.

The junior high teacher shifted his weight. "I kind of like the curriculum that we use right now."

"Yeah," the third grade teacher said, "it's easy to prepare and all the kids like it."

Everyone nodded.

"I . . . I don't understand," the superintendent gulped. "Are you saying that you want to stick with what we've got?"

"If it ain't broke," the fifth and sixth grade teacher huffed, "don't fix it."

■

Faith Redeemer Fellowship was facing another financial crisis. Unless a miracle happened, the small congregation would not have enough money to pay this year's bills. A potentially divisive solution presented itself. The church could take the money they annually gave to foreign missions and use it for their operating expenses. But over half the congregation, not to mention a majority of the board members, were violently opposed to such an idea. Pastor Jennifer Hiller knew she had an uphill fight on her hands. She expended a great deal of time and energy putting together a twelve-page study paper for the board which covered the nature of missions, tithing, principles of New Testament giving, parachurch organizations, and whether churches had a biblical obligation to give away some of what they collected. The conclusion of the paper stated that because Faith Redeemer Fellowship was a valid mission in and of itself, it was perfectly okay to use money that was budgeted for foreign missions to keep the church going.

To Jennifer's delight, the board approved her report and adopted her conclusion as their official standard operating procedure. The vote was unanimous. Jennifer went home that night elated and relieved.

At the next board meeting, however, the treasurer raised a concern. "I've just been mailed the winter oil bill and, ladies and gentlemen, we don't have the money to pay it."

"Excuse me," Jennifer offered, "but according to your financial report, we have an extra thousand dollars in the bank."

"That's our missions money. I can't pay the oil bill with that!"

"But we voted to. . . ."

"Pastor," another member broke in, "the Lord won't bless us if we don't give to his causes."

Still another member spoke up, admonishing the treasurer that he had forgotten what the board decided at their last meeting.

"I don't care what we decided. I'm not signing our mission money over to the oil company!" the treasurer yelled.

The room quickly split into two camps, each trying to out argue the other. Finally a motion was made to reconsider the pastor's report. This time around, the report was rejected.

Jennifer angrily sped home after the meeting. "I can't believe this!" she thought. "We're right back to square one. They essentially told me that my teaching is worthless. Fine! Let them solve their own problems. I'm through with them. I'm seeking another call."

In each of the incidents above, leaders learned the hard way that effort, logic, appeals to authority (even the Scriptures), and clear presentations often lead, ultimately, nowhere. People in small churches don't appreciate and reward rationality the same way seminary professors do. In fact, in the stories above people acted irrationally. It didn't matter what the leader said and did. The result would have been the same. Why is this the case? What makes people act irrationally when dealing with church issues?

For one thing, people are sinners. If you're in the ministry, you are pastoring a congregation of fallen men and women. If the sinful Israelites rejected God without any good reason (Hosea 11:1–7; Jeremiah 3:6–10), then sinners in your congregation will, at times, reject you and your ideas for no good reason. In fact, sometimes when people are acting irrationally they are just displaying their cursedness, pure and simple.

We also need to recognize that our culture predisposes people to irrationality. Western culture considers the most important questions to be not "Is this idea true?" or "Does this proposal have merit?" but "How do I feel about this?" and "Do I really want to accept it?"[4] Small-church members live not only within the American culture, but also within the culture of the small church. This culture will be described in detail in Chapter 3, but suffice it to say here that it predisposes people to sentimentality rather than rationality, to habit rather than purpose.

In the small church, there is no guarantee that boards and committees will act rationally. People are often voted into office because they have seniority in the congregation, are heavy financial contributors, or are just plain available. Whether or not they fit the biblical qualifications for church office is beside the point. Being experienced in the give-and-take of church politics is considered a plus, but not necessary. It often boils down to "Who wants the job?" Church boards can be made up of people who are popular in the congregation but who have never learned to calmly and logically discuss issues.

When men and women come to a church business meeting, they often aren't coming with a neutral mindset, wanting to hear all the facts on both sides before they make up their minds about an issue. In a small church, where board and committee members know each other well and have been together for years, it's likely that many "mini-meetings" have already occurred over the phone, at family picnics, at the supermarket, in the church parking lot, etc. before the scheduled meeting takes place. Therefore, people assemble with their minds already made up, not to search for the truth together.

People also attend the meetings to push their own agendas. For example, Sarah Rogers believes that the sanctuary needs a new carpet, but so far she hasn't been able to convince anyone else. Therefore, Sarah will vote against spending money to buy new toys for the nursery because in her

mind, that money is being set aside for the carpet she'll convince the church to get someday.

When men and women walk into the meeting room, they
are carrying invisible emotional baggage that will affect their
thoughts and their conduct. George White may be pushed
around by his boss, nagged by his wife, and ignored by his
teenage children. He may feel like a little man in the outside
world, but the one place where he has influence is the church
board. And he will definitely make his voice heard.

Even positive baggage and pleasant memories can cause
people to go against reason. John and Lydia Smith will vote
against revamping a dying Sunday school program because
the present department was set up years ago by beloved
Grandma Nelson, a matronly woman who led many children
(some of whom are now voting-age adults) to Christ. Nobody
wants to hurt Grandma Nelson's feelings.

People also come to business meetings for reasons other
than doing business. Sometimes they are really there to see
friends, catch up on the latest news, and get out of the house
for a while. Pastors may be annoyed at how much small talk
goes on at meetings, but laypeople may become annoyed
when the pastor tries to move ahead with the meeting's stated
purpose. Some laypeople are actually happy when special
meetings have to be called and projects drag on for months.
It gives them that much more time to be together.

How do leaders respond when confronted with irrational
people and situations in which logic doesn't seem to help?
Unfortunately, they often take one of two equally destructive
actions.

Some pastors throw themselves into the research and
report process all the more. This makes sense in light of the
academic training they've received. After all, in school if you
want to turn a C into an A, what do you do? You study harder.

There is certainly nothing wrong with hard work. It is
wrong, however, to believe that hard work will automatically

insure that you will be well-liked, respected, rewarded, and successful. Many leaders live with a terrible burden of guilt.

— "Since Elder Jones and I can't seem to get along, I must not be putting enough effort into the relationship."

— "I must be failing to make clear the biblical mandate to help the poor, or else why would the board keep turning down my proposal for a food pantry?"

— "It's my fault I can't move this church forward. If I were a stronger leader, my church would break the two-hundred barrier, develop a meaningful community outreach, have that new fellowship hall we need, etc." After all, church growth conferences and books make it clear that the buck stops at the leader's door.

But is this true? Don't we have to take into account sin and the fallen world in which we minister? The apostle Paul had colleagues desert him (2 Timothy 4:9–11, 16), saw a church he founded turn away from the Gospel (see the book of Galatians), and had Christians criticize his style of preaching and question his spiritual authority (2 Corinthians 10:1, 10; 11:5–6). Does this mean that he must have been a weak leader or that he didn't work hard enough in his ministry? Of course not! Neither is it necessarily true that when you face opposition or failure, something must be wrong with you and your style of ministry.

It is also not necessarily that you need to work harder. An electrical engineer friend of mine once put in sixty-five hours a week for three weeks at the computer firm where he worked. There was a glitch in a product that the company wanted to market, and it was his job to find and correct the problem. I felt sorry for him as I watched him stumble bleary-eyed to church and heard his family's lament, "We never see him anymore." But the poor man couldn't say "no" to the company. They had hired him for his expertise in the area, and they expected him to stay on the job until the problem was solved. The company knew the problem could and would be solved if concentration and effort were applied to it. Many pastors have the same viewpoint as the company. They know they have been hired for their expertise and believe they must put in the hours, the concentration, and the effort to solve any and all problems that arise in the church. And so they become workaholics, destroying themselves and their families. They fail to realize that they, unlike my friend, are not working within the orderly worlds of science and logic but are working with sinful, emotional, and sometimes irrational people. As a result, there will be some problems they won't be able to solve, no matter how hard they work on them. The key to surviving and thriving in the small church is not to work harder, but to work smarter. The smarter way is explained in Parts 2 and 3 of this book.

Other leaders, having found out the hard way that effort doesn't necessarily reap dividends, decide to quit making any effort. Although they keep their positions, they really don't have any hope that they can take a congregation anywhere it doesn't already want to go. Leadership is a joke, so why lead? Some pastors continue to preach and preside at church meetings, but they have internally distanced themselves from their congregations. The pastorate, instead of being a calling, becomes merely a job. And if that job is dull and unfulfilling, they will find fulfillment elsewhere. Pastors become passionate about golf, community theater, the town council, the Red Cross, anything but the church. If their workaday world is depressing, so what? They are not unlike so many other Americans who have to labor at jobs they don't like in order to make ends meet and have money to pursue the hobbies that really make life worthwhile. These pastors have learned, "Don't expect much and you won't be disappointed." And so they don't expect much when it comes to their congregations. They dream no dreams, have no goals, hold onto no hope.

They are just there on the job, putting in forty hours and then it's out the door. None of Paul's sleepless nights or inward burning over their congregation's sins for them (2 Corinthians 11:27–29). You can't do anything to really change people or churches anyway, so why give yourself an ulcer trying?

It's dangerous when a leader begins to feel this way. It shows that for him or her, faith in God and his transforming power is virtually nonexistent. "God may be able to take me to heaven, but he can't do much about this bride of his." Pastors increasingly find themselves loving the things of this world more genuinely than their brothers and sisters in Christ (1 John 2:9–10, 15–17). Let's remember that Jesus reserved one of his most graphic judgments for lukewarm Christians (Revelation 3:15–16).

It's unfortunate that leaders give up on the church when what they really need to do is give up on the idea that effort in the same areas that brought success in school—study, writing, researching, consulting authorities, directed reflection, etc.—will earn them an A grade when it comes to ministering in small churches. There is a way to get the A, but it is more relational than rational, and, on the surface, more intuitive than intentional. It is a way that demands the leader be more lover than boss and more participant than manager. One of my seminary professors said that it was a mystery to him why some of his best and brightest students bombed out in the ministry while students who struggled through to the M.Div. with Bs and Cs often pastor the most vital, exciting churches. Well, consider the mystery solved. Those who get lower grades usually are the ones who spend more time with people than with books. The education they receive from their friends and acquaintances is perfect preparation for the ministry. They are in the people business.[5] It is knowing, understanding, appreciating, and dealing with people that will determine whether you make it as a small-church leader or not.

PART TWO

The Tribe in the Pew

CHAPTER THREE

Family Resemblances

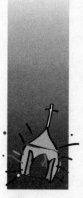

There are two things you have to understand about the small congregations in my area. First, they are more interested in the church building than they are in the church triumphant. Second, when they say they want church growth, they aren't saying that they want new people to join. What they really mean is that they wish that all the beloved members who have died or moved away could, by a miracle of God, be transported back to the sanctuary and take their rightful places in the pews again.
—a pastoral colleague

One can learn about small churches by observing a large extended family celebrating the holiday season. Nobody in the family ever has to ask, "Where's Thanksgiving dinner this year?" Everyone knows that it's always at Aunt Mary and Uncle Bill's. There's no need to coordinate who's going to bring what. Aunt Lisa always brings her famous stuffing. Cousin Marty bakes the pies. In fact, it just wouldn't be Thanksgiving without all the traditional delicacies made by the usual people. The schedule for Thanksgiving Day is the same as it has always been: everyone arrives between noon and two; dinner is at half-past two; after dinner some watch football while others help clean up (the same people do the same duties every year); the kids go out in the backyard to play; there's no formal supper hour, everyone can "graze" on leftovers at their leisure. At night, back in their own homes, the family members sigh contentedly before drifting off to sleep. "What a nice day," they think. "It's good to get the family together."

Christmas is more of the same. On Christmas Eve everybody heads over to Aunt Nan's for supper, eggnog, and carols around the fireplace. One year, Aunt Nan was sick and couldn't host the traditional gathering. Everyone said that it had been really hard to get into the Christmas spirit that year. On Christmas Day, it's off to Grandpa and Grandma's. The family arrives from half-past ten to noon, helping themselves to the munchies Grandma prepared. From noon until two, there's the gift exchange. The last gifts to be opened are the ones for Grandma and Grandpa. The whole room quiets down and everyone focuses on them. "Ooohs" and "aaahs" come at appropriate moments. After the last gift is unwrapped, Aunt Amy always gives a little speech about how precious Grandma and Grandpa are and how lucky the family is to have them. Everyone applauds and then it's on to Christmas dinner (with familiar favorites like Uncle Larry's Swedish meatballs, Cousin Sue's pumpkin bread, etc.). The remainder of the day is spent sitting back and "shooting the breeze" while the kids play underfoot with their new toys.

At the gathering, Uncle Ken will go into a rambling, semi-coherent monologue about left-wing politics, but nobody ever pays him any mind. "That's just Uncle Ken." And nobody will bring up the feud Aunts Lisa and Mary are having or the fact that Cousin Sue has an alcohol problem and is dating a married man. Everybody knows about these problems but what can you do? Besides, it would wreck the mood to bring them up. The purpose of the holidays is to enjoy being together, not to intrude into one another's personal lives.

On New Year's Eve and New Year's Day, the family is pretty much on its own. Getting together was never a big deal on these dates. Last year, a few of the younger cousins tried to organize a party, but nothing ever came of it. No, family members are used to and content with staying in their own homes and resting up for the start of another year.

There are always a few nonfamily members at the holiday gatherings. Some of the cousins bring dates. The family is always polite to them, but mostly it just ignores them and converses about people and subjects the newcomers know nothing about. In fact, if the truth be told, there's a certain unspoken, below-the-surface resentment of the dates. "Why do they really have to be here? This is a family time, after all." And sometimes the dates disturb the celebration, like last year when one of them suggested that the adults try out Cousin Kim's new Trivial Pursuit game. That was disrespectful to Grandpa and Grandma—they hadn't opened their gifts yet. It wouldn't do for a group of young folks to up and leave the room. Besides, with dinner and the visiting afterwards, there is no time for game-playing. Dates were necessary evils, everybody guessed, but the get-togethers would probably be better if they weren't there.

―――

Many models have been proposed to help define the small church. Small churches have been compared to "one big happy family,"[1] a tribal folk society,[2] and a clan.[3] All of these pictures have common elements. They all describe a group who are determined to stay together, who work to preserve their traditions, who are led by a few key figures, and who are often suspicious, if not contemptuous, of outsiders. This is the small church. Let us consider each of these characteristics in turn.

1. *The small church is a group determined to stay together.* The question the small church asks when they consider a new program or a change of any sort is not, "Is it the right thing to do?" but "Will this upset anybody?" The goal of the small church is to make sure their members remain happy enough that they continue to attend the "family gatherings." A pastor who left a staff position at a megachurch to pastor a

small congregation remarked that she was astonished at all the complaining she heard about every little thing. She was equally astonished that her board expected her to listen to every complaint. The board itself gave equal weight to the complaints of those who just showed up on Sunday and those of the hardest-working members of the congregation. She had been used to ministering in a system where only superiors had the right to put the brakes on ideas, not Gladys Jones who sits in the third row. The fact is that anyone in the small church has the power to put the brakes on any idea, if he or she complains loudly enough. Complaints are listened to because the goal of the church is not to move ahead but to keep everyone happy.

This means that church discipline in the small church is a real problem. Pastors have found that small churches won't confront individuals or families with their sins because, "It's just going to make them mad. We could wind up losing them and a lot of their friends if we pursue this issue." They also feel that if you bring up someone's sin, you are rude and unaccepting. After all, aren't Christians called to love one another? "Pastor, why can't you just love and accept him the way he is? At least he's still coming to church!" The fact that one still attends the "family gatherings" covers a multitude of sins. If the pastor points out that sinful attitudes in the congregation would drive away potential new members, the response is, "If they can't put up with us, then who needs them? Nobody's perfect, you know!" The goal of the group's leaders is not so much to help members mature as Christians as it is to make sure they remain in the church.

Pastors and leaders who are bursting at the seams with new ideas often forget this. Because their ideas are constantly voted down, they assume that the small church has no real goals and/or is afraid to do the hard work necessary to advance the kingdom of God. However, the small church is usually working very hard at its goal—keeping its little part of the kingdom in one piece. When leaders say, "The problem with this church is that it has grown fat and lazy," the often incredulous response from people like the vice president of the board or the Sunday school superintendent is, "What do you mean? Why just last night I spent three hours on the phone with Hal trying to get him to simmer down about the new hymnals. And I had to be up at 6:00 A.M. to go to work. You don't think I'm doing enough? You want me, somehow, to do more? Forget it!"

2. *The small church is a group that works to preserve their traditions.* Just as Thanksgiving wouldn't be the same without the trip to Aunt Mary and Uncle Bill's, so a church "just isn't the same somehow" when things aren't the way they've always been for years and years. In fact when too much change takes place, the small church makes the moral judgment that things aren't right anymore.[4] This judgment is expressed in a variety of ways:

— "I just don't sense God's presence here like I used to."
— "This church doesn't feel like home anymore."
— "I was growing more under Pastor Previous' ministry."

However it's expressed, the message to the leader is, "Because you've changed my world, you've committed a mortal sin."

A new pastor was given the green light to try a new Easter sunrise service. "After all, we do the same thing every year. Might be nice to try something different," he was told. As Easter approached, however, the pastor began to receive phone calls.

— "Pastor, did anyone mention that the Sunday school kids always sing during the service? They expect to do it, so if it's not too much trouble, could you pencil it in?"

— "We always ended the sunrise service by holding
hands and singing the doxology. A lot of people, myself
included, find that really meaningful. Last year, I swear
I had chills running up and down my spine. Can we do
that again this year?"

And so it went until finally the service was pretty much
what the people were used to. Everyone said it was very moving. Somehow the pastor wasn't surprised. What was surpris-
ing was that the green light had changed to red so quickly.
More than one pastor has discovered that the small church
who assured him or her during the candidating process that
they were ready to change turned out to be as tradition-bound
as ever once the new minister was on the field.

Because tradition is so important, the church building is
also important. It is the traditional family home, the place
where many pleasant memories live. To preserve the memories, the church must preserve the building. This is why so
much time at board meetings is taken up with details about
building maintenance: "Did everybody notice that one of the
lights in the fellowship hall is out?"

"How are we going to decide what color the new sanctuary carpet should be?"

"When was the last time the roof was repaired?" Often
the group is more concerned about these areas than about
how the congregation is maturing spiritually.

In fact, as long as a congregation is keeping up their facilities, they often view themselves as a success regardless of
whatever else they do or don't do. At a judicatory meeting, a
dying congregation of twelve senior citizens praised the Lord
that it was able to install a new boiler in the church building.
"God always comes through with the money to do his work,"
one of the elders stated. Nobody brought up the fact that the
group was doing absolutely nothing for outreach and had, in
fact, recently chased away a young couple with children who

had been attending there. No, the important thing was that tradition had been preserved. Mission accomplished.

3. *The small church is a group led by a few key figures.* Families have their respected matriarchs and patriarchs. So does the small church. They are often the people who have seemingly been around forever. Sometimes they are younger members who are involved in everything the church has going on. But whatever their age, they are the ones others in the congregation look to for leadership and guidance (even if they don't hold an elected office in the organization). When key figures talk, everybody listens. When a new idea is brought up at a board meeting, everyone looks over at the key figure to see how he or she is reacting to it. If the key figure is not a member of the board, someone will suggest, "Let's talk to Don about this and see what his feelings are." No important decisions are ever made while key figures are away on vacation. More than one pastor has been frustrated that boards put everything on hold "until Mary gets here." Key figures are those who the pastor must have on his or her side if anything is going to happen in a church. Conversely, once the pastor upsets or offends a key figure, the pastor's days are numbered.

Church growth and leadership expert John Maxwell (currently the pastor of a megachurch) was able to have a very successful ministry in a small-town, small-membership church because he recognized one man as a tribal leader of sorts. Before the board meetings, Maxwell would "just drop by" the man's house and discuss the church's concerns. At the board meeting, Maxwell would sit back and let the key figure take over. New ideas passed with no dissension at all.[5]

On the other hand, another pastor disagreed with a key figure over how the Sunday school department should be structured, a figure who had been responsible for leading many in the congregation to the Lord. In less than a year, the pastor was forced to seek another call. Still another pastor couldn't understand why the elders wouldn't do anything about a married woman in the church who was sending him love letters. Then he realized that she belonged to one of the founding families of the congregation. Key figures can get away with almost anything.

4. *The small church is a group who are often suspicious, if not contemptuous, of outsiders.* Unfortunately, even new members of the congregation are viewed as outsiders. This is understandable given the three characteristics described above. New members haven't been around long enough to demonstrate that they are really going to stay with the group come what may. Small churches have often "seen them come and seen them go" (the fact that often people are driven from the church by the distrustful attitudes they encounter never occurs to the small congregation). New members don't understand the groups' "sacred" traditions and aren't committed to upholding and defending them. New members don't know about or operate in the church's power structure. In fact, energetic, enthusiastic, charismatic new members can be viewed as threats to the powers that be.

Suspicion and contempt express themselves in a number of ways. Many small churches will say that they want to grow, yet when visitors attend the worship service nobody bothers to greet, welcome, or even talk to them. People who have been attending for a couple of years are still referred to as, "That new family who sits in the third row—oh, you know, what's-their-names."

The pastor receives his or her share of suspicion and contempt as well because the pastor is the most potentially dangerous newcomer there is. The status quo is threatened by this stranger who people will listen to; therefore, action must be taken at once. Small-church boards often view keeping the pastor in line as their unwritten job description. Some will even say as much to the pastor's face. One board chose several young, inexperienced candidates in a row to pastor their church, despite the fact that they felt each candidate had some serious faults. The board's reasoning was, "We can train these pastors to be what they need to be" (read instead, "what we want them to be"). Is it any wonder then that in eleven years, this church went through four pastors?

Other churches are not as blatant in their attempts to control their pastors, but attempt to control them they will. Certain "friendly" members of the board will often take the pastor aside to explain to him or her that, "you just have to understand the way things work around here."

— "Although you didn't mean to, Pastor, that announcement you put in the newsletter offended some people."
— "Pastor, you're trying too much, too fast. We think you should slow down some or else you might burn us out."
— "Don't get me wrong, Pastor, you have a good idea, but we tried something like it before, and it just didn't work."

Whatever words are used, the message comes through loud and clear, "Stranger, don't disturb our family. Don't change our traditions. Don't usurp power from our leaders."

The high-powered pastor who enters the small church ready to take the reigns and lead is in for a real shock. The small church quite simply won't let you. And maybe it shouldn't. How would you like a stranger to come into your house and start telling you how to run your family? C. Peter Wagner points out that church leadership is earned. He writes,

... it is not automatic that people will follow a pastor just because he or she has the title. When you accept a call to an existing church you are on probation usually for three to six years. During that period of time, the people in the church are in the process of deciding one thing above all— whether or not you are their servant. This is what is behind

Lyle Schaller's observation that the productive years of a given pastorate begin around years four, five, or six. It takes that long to earn your right to lead by proving that you are a servant.[6]

Before you can ever be a leader in a small church, you must be a friend. Roy M. Oswald feels strongly "that clergy new to their congregations should spend six to nine months being little more than a lover and a historian."[7] In small churches, the time period is usually much longer. The congregation needs the pastor to fit in and become one of the family before they will listen to him or her. The pastor may, in time, become a leader in fact as well as in name, but this will only happen as the congregation comes to accept the pastor as a "tribal leader" instead of viewing him or her as an outsider who is trying to take over.

Pastors and leaders who want to survive and thrive in small churches should adopt a missionary model for their ministries. Like missionaries in foreign fields, small-church leaders are often entering a culture that is not their own. They have an important message to bring. They have changes they want to see implemented in people's lifestyles. But they know that their message will go unheard and changes will go unmade if they are not first accepted and trusted by those to whom they minister. Small-church leaders, like missionaries, need to learn about the people, customs, laws, philosophy, and government of the land. As much as possible, they need to work within existing structures and with prevailing mindsets in order to make inroads for the Gospel.

CHAPTER FOUR

One of the Gang

"We loved you so much that we were delighted to share with you not only the gospel of God but our lives as well, because you had become so dear to us."

—The apostle Paul to the church in Thessalonica (1 Thessalonians 2:8)

"You know that those who are regarded as rulers of the Gentiles lord it over them, and their high officials exercise authority over them. Not so with you. Instead, whoever wants to become great among you must be your servant, and whoever wants to be first must be slave of all. For even the Son of Man did not come to be served, but to serve, and to give his life as a ransom for many."

—Jesus Christ (Mark 10:42–45)

Church-growth experts maintain that "everything rises and falls on leadership." In the small church, however, everything rises and falls on relationship. People in small congregations will not follow one who is perceived to be an outsider. Small congregations don't want an outside expert to come in and fix all their problems. They want a close friend who can occasionally offer some helpful advice. Small-church leaders must seek to become accepted as "one of the gang" by the members of the congregation.

This acceptance is difficult for pastors to achieve because the very nature of their office separates them from the people in the pews. In the minds of many small-church members, pastors are up on pedestals. A pastor's prayers are thought to have more effect than those of the layperson. Pastors are supposed to be closer than most to what God wants a man or woman to be. While the pastor may not be quite a saint, he or she is seen to be something more than merely human. To further complicate matters, the pastor is usually someone from somewhere else who moves into the community for a time and then leaves. Everyone knows that the pastor isn't putting down roots and so isn't really "one of us." A pastor's relationship with a congregation is always temporary. The congregation says, "We've seen them come and we've seen them go, but the *real church* is made up of those of us who will always be here." One pastor had been with a small church for twenty years and even bought his own house in town. Still, when he retired he believed that he and his wife would have to worship elsewhere so as not to hinder the work of the new minister.

It's also difficult for new lay leaders to be completely accepted by the church. A new board member has no shared history with the other members. They have the sort of camaraderie which only comes from having been through numerous crises together. They can share war stories and compare battle scars while the new member can only sit there and say nothing. They know they can handle the pressures of the give-and-take of church politics and deal with the problems of keeping a small church going, but the new member has yet to have his or her mettle tested. So new members often find themselves "out of the loop"—not contacted by phone or stopped in the parking lot for the informal "board meetings before and after the board meeting" where the real business of the congregation is conducted.

New lay leaders are often viewed with suspicion and skepticism. In the small church one may hear, "It's great that young Mrs. Blake volunteered to be the new Sunday school superintendent, but I wonder if she really understands how our department runs." The Sunday school department has their own way of doing things, and while it isn't written down anywhere on paper, it's written on the hearts and minds of those involved. Mrs. Penn always leads the opening exercises, and while they are a bit old-fashioned, no one wants to offend her by suggesting changes. Is Mrs. Blake aware that no Sunday school money is ever used to purchase the award Bibles given to the third-graders? Will Mrs. Blake "play by the rules" (even those she doesn't know about) or will she upset the apple cart? The teachers take a "wait and see" attitude toward Mrs. Blake and unconsciously keep her at arm's length.

How then can a leader work toward acceptance? First, the leader must realize that it really does take work—and sacrifice. Pastor Jameson was really looking forward to vacation. Though his family couldn't afford to go anywhere, it was going to be so nice to spend time together without being interrupted by phone calls. However, on the first day of his vacation he noticed a fire truck pulling into the church parking lot. He ran over and found volunteer fire fighters and church members hard at work. A water pipe had burst. Now there was water to be pumped out, books and equipment to be saved, damage to be assessed, and decisions to be made. Pastor Jameson stayed and pitched in. Although he was on vacation, he heard himself saying, "We're going to be in town this week. If there's anything else I can do, or if you need my input on anything, don't hesitate to call." After all, would a member of a family refuse to help out during a family crisis just because he or she was on vacation? Pastor Jameson had learned long ago that in order to be accepted by a small congregation as an insider, a leader must think and act as though he or she already is an insider. There are many practical ways to do this.

First, a leader must put on a positive attitude about his or her group. Instead of coming to committee meetings and church gatherings with a list of everything wrong that needs to be fixed, the leader should exude an aura of being comfortable and at home with the way things are. "This is my church and I love it. Sure, there are some problems, but nothing major is wrong. I'm confident that all of the problems will be taken care of in time." Would a new son- or daughter-in-law be accepted as one of the family if it seemed that all he or she ever did was find fault with it? Neither will you as a leader be accepted if it seems to the congregation as if all you ever do is complain.

The church leader should attend as many of the church gatherings as he or she possibly can. Lay leaders who only come to committee meetings and Sunday morning worship services, while skipping Bible studies and fellowship activities, need not wonder why they can never break into the inner circle of the congregation. Pastors who won't at least put in appearances at church fund-raisers, or stop in when people in the congregation are having a church "fix it" day to see how it's going, can send a negative message to the congregation loudly and clearly. "I'm not one of you. The things that are important to you don't concern me in the slightest." Leaders must be actively involved in the life of the congregation and act as though they enjoy it.

But can one be a sincere Christian leader if one has to "act as if" and try to "exude an aura"? Must leaders be phonies? No, but leaders must put others' desires and feelings ahead of their own in order to advance the cause of Christ. This is thoroughly biblical (Romans 12:14–16; Philippians 2:1–4). As a pastor, it's something I have to do all the time.

For example, Sunday night is usually the worst time of the week for me. After a day of ministering and meeting with needy people, I am utterly spent. All I want to do is go to bed, yet I'm also keyed up after a day of being "on" all the time. I feel irritable. My nerves are on edge. The last thing I want to happen on Sunday night is for the phone to ring. I just want to be left alone. Still, if the phone does ring, I find myself answering it with a cheerful voice and assuring the person on the other end of the line that, no, he or she isn't disturbing me—after all, that's what I'm here for. Even as I say it, I know I don't mean it (and so does my wife). I'm merely playing the role that's expected of me as a pastor.

Sunday mornings are little better than Sunday evenings. I am one of those unfortunate pastors who has to spend hours on the toilet before the worship service starts. I often arrive at the church feeling drained and a little nauseous. But, of course, I can't make a beeline for our church lounge in order to flop down on the couch and take a nap. I don't even tell anyone that I'm not feeling well. Instead, I put on my, "It's good to see you all and to be here to worship the Lord with you" air and voice.

Is the Lord angry at me because at times I am less than sincere? Would the cause of Christ really be better served if I was honest with my Sunday night caller? "Right about now, I could care less about the fact that your brother-in-law's friend's uncle is in the hospital. All I feel like doing is taking off my head and drop kicking it through a goal post!" Would it be more honoring to God if I started out the worship service by saying, "Can you hear that? It's my intestines rumbling. Yeah, my irritable bowel syndrome is acting up again, but I probably can make it through the service as long as the special music and the prayer requests don't run too long."

When God commands us to love our neighbor in the same way that we love ourselves, is he commanding us to feel a certain way toward our neighbor or to act in a certain way toward our neighbor? It is a fact of life that feelings follow actions. This is why I counsel couples who believe that the magic is gone to stay committed to each other and keep acting as though they enjoy being married. The magic will come back. As I act as though I'm entering into my caller's problem, I find myself feeling concern and compassion. As I act as though it's good to be in church on Sunday morning, lo and behold, I find that it *is* good to be there.[1]

If leaders act as though they are insiders, eventually they will feel like insiders. Others will begin to accept them as insiders. This won't happen overnight. Acceptance takes time. Some leaders give up too soon. Leaders must be in prayer for patience and perseverance.

Another key to acceptance is simply being willing to spend time with members of the church. This sounds obvious, but more than one leader has bristled when answering phone calls takes him or her away from "the real work of the ministry"—reading church-growth books, planning an outreach strategy to reach the Generation Xers who hang out at the mall, and drafting a five-year plan to reorganize the church. A pastor often resents a congregation's expectation that he or she pop into the local diner or post office at least three times a week to chat awhile with the folks who are there. It seems like such a waste of valuable time! In reality, however, it is an extremely wise use of time. Not only does it show members of the congregation that you care for and respect them as individuals, it also makes it easier for you to gain the acceptance needed if your ideas are ever going to go anywhere. Your five-year plan is destined for "the circular file" if the congregation thinks you aren't friendly. Remember that the members of the church talk to each other for hours on the phone and chew the fat at the local meeting places. If you are willing to do these things too, then you'll be seen as fitting right in.

How a leader handles conflict will also determine whether or not he or she is accepted as "one of the gang."[2] In small-church conflicts, the most important thing for leaders to work toward is not to be proven right or to have their ideas and plans approved. The most important thing for leaders to work toward is restoring any broken relationships with others in the church. If your relationships are restored then even if your idea isn't adopted now, there's still a chance that it will be sometime in the future. If relationships aren't healed then even if others in the church are grudgingly made to see things your way now, you will be branded an "outsider" or even an "enemy," and there will be trouble for you down the road. You may win the battle, but lose the war.

Leaders forget that the Bible commands them to: work for unity (Ephesians 4:1–3); humbly "consider others better than yourselves" (Philippians 2:1–4); "submit to one another" (Ephesians 5:21); and work toward agreements with others in the church (Philippians 4:2–3). Instead, leaders often focus exclusively on "standing firm for the truth," "exercising tough love," and "fighting for what's right for this church." While these things are important, the Bible's teaching, taken as a whole, shows us that relationships are equally important and that compromise isn't always a dirty word. In Matthew 19:3–8 Jesus teaches that even part of the inspired Old Testament law was a compromise on Moses' (and the Lord's) part because of the Israelite's spiritual state at the time! Christians are called to do all in their power to live at peace with others (Romans 12:18; Matthew 5:23–26). This will, of necessity at times, involve compromise. Small-church leaders have to be willing to make compromises and to put some of their ideas "on the shelf" for awhile. They will have to trust that God will eventually bring people around (Philippians 3:15) without constant hammering and pressure from the leaders. They will have to walk away from some fights, refusing to participate (2 Timothy 2:23–26; Proverbs 26:4). And leaders need to do all these things in good conscience, instead of feeling guilty that they are somehow letting down the cause of God and Truth because they refuse to fight.

Unfortunately some leaders, whether because of temperament, upbringing, or a faulty understanding of Scripture, believe that if they aren't fighting with someone over something, they aren't doing God's work. And, to be honest, some people simply enjoy fighting. It's easier and sometimes more fun and immediately gratifying to spend time and energy fighting and putting enemies "down" than it is to spend it practicing the spiritual disciplines, helping the poor, or evangelizing. A pastor who served in a church that had a reputation for bucking the denomination once said to me, "Ironically, the worst thing in the world for my congregation would be if the denomination started seeing things their way. They wouldn't have anyone to fight anymore, and fighting is their favorite sport. They would purposely go looking for other adversaries, looking for fights to pick. They would probably turn on each other or on me." Small-church leaders must purposely go looking to make friends, not to ferret out enemies.

During a conflict, a small-church leader must reassure the members of the congregation that he or she still wants to be friends. He or she must project and even verbalize an attitude of, "I'm trying to find a solution to this problem that we can all live with." Many small churches don't expect their pastors to stay around very long, and so they live in fear that the latest crisis will be the one that sends the pastor packing. Pastors can alleviate that fear by letting people know that the current problem isn't enough to make him or her break off the relationship he or she has with the congregation. Once that fear is dealt with, everyone can breathe easier and focus all their energies on actually solving the problem rather than on worrying about where the next pastor will come from. Likewise, lay leaders must not give the impression that they are ready to resign from the board, the Sunday school department, the choir, or the missions committee the minute things aren't going their way. Instead, they must show others in the small church that "We're in this thing together and I'll stick it out as long as you all will." In this way, conflict can be the means that God uses to actually draw leaders and congregations closer together.

To stop a conflict from driving you and your congregation farther apart, you must make sure that you keep a proper perspective on yourself, on others, and on the problems causing the conflict. You must remember that you are not God's infallible instrument sent to guide your congregation. If a leader like Peter could be wrong and need correction (Galatians 2:11–14), isn't it possible that you could be wrong also, at least occasionally? If the apostle Paul felt he had to submit his message to others to make sure that he had rightly understood the Gospel (Galatians 2:1–10), isn't it wise to submit your ideas to others in order to make sure you have really understood what God wants to do in your congregation?

Others may have valuable insights to offer and it is wise to seek their counsel (Proverbs 11:14; 18:17). Make sure that you are listening to what "the opposition" is saying. It's just possible that they may be right and you may be wrong. Remember, too, that "the opposition" are valued and important members of the body of Christ (1 Corinthians 12) and shouldn't be viewed as "unrepentant enemies of God who are standing in the way of his kingdom's advance." It's helpful to put yourself in "the opposition's" shoes and try to look at the situation as they see it. Look for factors in small-church culture or personal backgrounds which may be influencing their thoughts. True, they may be living in the past or not looking at the big picture. They may even be misguided. Does this necessarily mean they are sinful? Think twice before pronouncing judgment on God's people.

Few problems that arise in the small church are as earth-shattering as they first appear. Whichever way they are resolved, chances are that the small congregation will still be there next year and that the universal church of Jesus Christ won't crumble before the forces of hell. Once I attended a presbytery meeting held at a country church. Votes on several key issues didn't go the way I firmly believed they should. I stepped out for a breath of fresh air, feeling very depressed and defeated. It was then I noticed a herd of dairy cows grazing on a nearby hillside. As I watched them sleepily chewing their cud and swishing their tails, a feeling of peace came over me. I realized, "These cows couldn't care less about what just happened in our presbytery meeting. It's totally irrelevant to them. Their world is secure and it's much larger than the presbytery." Face it, unless you are voting on whether or not to construct neutron bombs in the church basement, very few of the decisions made in a small church will bring about the end of the world. But they could bring about the end of precious relationships. Do your best to prevent that from happening.

———

If the leader must try to keep relationships intact, compromise when necessary, be drawn closer to his or her people, and be accepted as "one of the gang," where then does the leading come in? Once accepted as an insider, how does a leader get the tradition-bound small church to accept new challenges and new direction? Won't suggestions for change be seen as a betrayal by those who thought the leader was happy and content in the local small church?

The answers to these questions are found in Part 3.

PART THREE

How Should We Then Lead?

CHAPTER FIVE

Let It Be

"Small church people (all folk society people, actually) do not like to waste time re-inventing the wheel. So most of what is done, or at least the way in which it is done, is done out of habit."
—Anthony Pappas[1]

In seminary my class heard missionary stories from Africa that shocked us—not because they were about headhunters or encounters with demonic witch doctors, but because they flew in the face of what we had always considered to be the right way of doing things.

We were told that whole tribes would convert to Christianity just because their chiefs told them to. As missionaries tried to witness to individual villages about Christ they would be told, "Talk to our chief about this. He's the wisest and most experienced man in the tribe. He's our trusted leader. It's up to him to decide what god we follow. If he decides that we should worship Jesus, we will. If he doesn't, we won't." And true to their word, if a chief converted to Christianity and ordered his people to do the same, they would.

When the professor was done recounting this, many hands shot up in the classroom. "But surely," our preprogrammed, evangelical minds protested, "those kinds of conversions weren't real! Every person must decide for himself or herself whether or not Jesus is Lord."

"That's not the way things work in tribal Africa," our professor said. "All I know is that the fruit of the Spirit began appearing in the people's lives along with a hunger for the Word of God and a thirst to encounter God in worship."

Speaking of worship, in tribal Africa the Sunday services are completely different from those in the Western world. For one thing, they have no starting or ending times. They begin early in the morning whenever a group gathers together, and they run continuously through the day, ending in the evening whenever there's nobody left to keep them going. Worshipers come and go as they please—arriving whenever they want, staying for as long as they want, leaving whenever they want, and coming back again later if they want. There's no prelude, call to worship, choir anthem, or benediction. Corporate singing, prayer, and testimonies fill the day. Whenever they feel led, preachers stand up and deliver messages, the lengths of which vary depending on the subjects. It's not unheard of for a preacher to give four or five different messages during the day.

If a missionary who came to the tribe locked himself in his study for twenty hours a week in order to prepare one twenty-minute Sunday morning message, he would be viewed as very strange indeed by the people. If a missionary became upset because worship didn't start at 10:00 A.M. to be followed by Sunday school at 11:15, she would be laughed at. If missionaries insisted on handing out *The Four Spiritual Laws* tracts and pressing for decisions for Christ, they would be ignored.

As our professor cautioned us, when one goes to another culture to plant a church, one must not predetermine what that church will look like. One must be willing to let a group express their faith in their own way. A missionary should not be out to build a church that he or she feels comfortable with but rather one in which the natives will feel at home.

A small-church leader ministers in the culture that was described in Chapter 3. He or she can't enter into the leadership role carrying all sorts of presuppositions (from books, seminars, observing other congregations, etc.) about what the ideal church looks like. The leader must find out "what Christianity looks like here." One of the goals leaders should have is to help the people be themselves—the best selves they can possibly be. To do this, a leader must determine what God was doing in the congregation before he or she arrived and/or assumed the reigns of leadership. Too many leaders express contempt for the past history of their groups. They flirt with pride and arrogance when they assume that God really wasn't doing much of anything before they arrived. God was just biding his time, waiting for the day when Super Leader would appear and drag the church into the Promised Land.

However, the Bible shows us that our God works through the personal and corporate histories of his people to accomplish his purposes. Jesus Christ came to be a godly king after the manner of David. David was a good king because he loved and followed the law given by Moses. Moses appeared on the scene as the instrument God used to fulfill his promise to Abraham. God's promise to Abraham was in fulfillment of God's words to the serpent, that from Eve's offspring would come one that would crush Satan's head. What God is doing now has its roots in what God was doing then. God may not be waiting for you to "cast a vision" for your congregation as much as he is waiting for you to catch the vision of where your church is already headed.

How can you determine where your group is headed? Ask them. As a leader in a small church you have an advantage that leaders in larger congregations don't have—you can have personal contact with every member of your congregation. Why not invite over a few families at a time for a potluck dinner, or dessert and coffee, and chat about the church? Be up front about the fact that you are having the families over to get to know them and to get a handle on what God wants you to do as a leader in the congregation. Let them know that sometime during the course of the evening you will be asking them the following questions:

> — How long have you been coming to this church? Why did you happen to attend that first time? What made you decide to stay?
> — What is one of your favorite memories about this church—it could be a person, an event, a program, or a moment when God really spoke to you?
> — Name one thing that you really appreciate about our church as it is now.
> — If it was totally up to you (and didn't need the approval of any boards or committees), what's one thing about our church that you would change immediately?

Make it clear that there will be a definite ending time for the evening. Some people won't show up if they think they will be hearing others ramble on all night. Also, let it be known that anybody can pass on answering any question. The purpose of the evening is to share thoughts together, not to embarrass others or put people on the spot. Nobody's answers will be attacked. The evening is for brainstorming and brain-dumping, not debating. Be careful to go down the membership list, making sure that every member and regular worship attender gets an invitation to one of your get-togethers (even if they turn the invitation down). Otherwise, the notion could spread that you are meeting with a cadre of your followers in order to plot a revolutionary takeover of the church. Keep these precautions in mind, and your dinners/desserts can be used by the Lord to give you a very clear picture of the congregation you serve.[2]

An equally important way to determine where God is taking your congregation is to simply make a list of what's being done now. While God does indeed move people's thoughts in certain directions and gives people a desire to be more of what he wants them to be, it's also true that "actions speak louder than words." In the small church a rule of thumb is, "If it wasn't there before you arrived, chances are good that it won't appear soon after your arrival." Old habits will be hard to break and new habits will be even harder to start. Many pastors have taken calls to small churches who really weren't doing much of anything for evangelism but were supposedly ready to go forward and were just waiting for the right leader to come and get things started. More than one pastor has become disappointed and bitterly frustrated when, two years after his or her arrival, the congregation still wasn't doing much of anything for evangelism. It's been truthfully stated that as a small-church leader, "you inherit more than you create." This fact doesn't have to cripple you, as we shall see, but it does have to be reckoned with.[3]

Another helpful thing to do is to identify the "chiefs" that you must convert and convince if anything is going to happen in the church. Write out an organizational chart for your church as it would appear ideally and officially "on paper." At the top of the chart, put the group or individual who is supposed to have the ultimate say over what happens in the congregation (board of elders, trustees, pastor, etc.). Below that, write down groups or individuals who give the most input to the group or individual named above (worship committee, church secretary, etc.). Then write the people or groups who give the most input to the ones immediately above (Sunday school teachers, choir members, etc.). Work your way on down until the last line of your chart says, "average members of the congregation." Next, write out a second chart—this time reflecting the church as it really is. On the new chart the top line may read, "church secretary, Mr. Goodrick, and the ladies fellowship." Next may come "the board of trustees and the choir director." The pastor may actually appear on the third or fourth line down! Compare your two lists. Noting the persons and groups listed on the first three lines of each will give you a clear picture of who the "chieftains" of the congregation are.

Having determined the power structure within your church and gotten a feeling for where the church has been and where they're going, you are now ready to put this knowledge to use and lead your congregation.

———— ▬ ————

The spiritual growth committee was frustrated. As part of their job description, they were supposed to "encourage the study of the Holy Scriptures by providing opportunities for members of the congregation to meet together to focus on God's Word." However when they scheduled a midweek Bible study, only three people showed up. When they tried to divide the congregation into home study and fellowship groups, the response was less than enthusiastic. People were too busy, didn't like their particular grouping, couldn't see the need, etc.

The committee was about ready to give up when one member joked at a meeting, "Let's face it. If you can't eat it, our people aren't interested in it. The only activity that's well attended around here is the potluck dinners."

"Hey, wait a minute!" another member brightened up. "Why can't we use that to our advantage?"

"Huh? I was just kidding around."

"I know, but you hit on an important point. If we want our Bible study program to have the most impact, why not run it at the time most people are here? Why not have a study hour immediately following a potluck supper?"

And that's just what they did. Once a month, they scheduled fellowship/learning dinners. After a potluck supper, the pastor would teach and lead a discussion on a biblical topic for an hour or an hour and a half. Everyone who attended always seemed to be enjoying it. The congregation saw that

Bible study wasn't so bad after all. Many of them began to show visible signs of growing in the faith.

The committee felt relieved, especially after the pastor told the group at one dinner, "What we're doing tonight is much the same sort of thing the early church did. Many of their gatherings centered around a shared meal. You might say that we're following a grand old tradition." And we all know how much small congregations love tradition!

———

First Presbyterian Church was sorry to see Pastor Franklin and his family leave. They all liked him very much, even though he was unable to bring any younger families into the church. They all, including Pastor Franklin, had high hopes when the graying congregation called a young man to be their minister. But somehow things just didn't pan out.

It wasn't that the church wasn't growing. Under Pastor Franklin's ministry, new members were joining. It's just that they were all "sixty-five-plus" years old, like the people who were already there. If that was the only kind of members the church could attract, the future looked bleak. In another twenty-five years, the congregation would probably cease to exist because too few members would be left alive to keep it going.

After Pastor Franklin settled into his new call, he continued to hear from his friends at First Presbyterian. The church was continuing to attract the over-sixty-five crowd. It continued to offer the kinds of activities that appealed to seniors—rummage sales, Saturday night card games, and picnics where the most strenuous activity was carrying a plate with three different pieces of pie back to one's seat. Pastor Franklin began to see in hindsight what God was doing at First Presbyterian. He was building up a church that could reach a segment of the population that is often ignored in the rush to minister to Baby Boomers and Baby Busters. Franklin hoped his friends could see that, too. He hoped they would stop feeling bad about themselves and start celebrating who they were.

———　■　———

When the Reverend Terry Yates first met the Sunday school superintendent of his new church, he felt he was meeting a living legend. Mrs. Mildred Westphal single-handedly started and defined the Sunday school program of the small congregation thirty-five years ago. And she had run it ever since.

One of the first things Mrs. Westphal asked Terry was, "Pastor, what do you think about vacation Bible school programs? Our last pastor, who everyone knows I didn't get along with, didn't think much of them, and so for the last six years we didn't have one. I think that's a shame, don't you? A church needs to reach the children of the community. I'd like to see us start VBS up again. Why, we used to fill the church for a week in July. That needs to happen again. Don't you agree?"

Terry's first impulse was to say, "Yes. In fact, I was planning to start a VBS this year." Instead, however, something made him say, "Mrs. Westphal, that's a great idea! We'd need to find someone to get it organized, though. Would you be willing to do it?"

Mrs. Westphal beamed. "Of course. I always used to run it. I'll round up the same teachers who did it before and we can use the Sonshine Soldiers curriculum. We've always had a good response with that." Suddenly, Mrs. Westphal lowered her eyes, hesitated, and then said softly and slowly, "Unless, of course, Pastor, you know of something you'd rather have us use."

Terry's pulse raced. He considered the Sonshine Soldiers material outdated and lacking in the interpretation of

Scripture on certain doctrines. Yet he knew that to verbalize this would cut his own throat. So he said, "I've always liked Let the Children Come myself. It's very colorful and the Bible stories really come alive in the classroom. But you would know best for us, seeing as how you've worked in the church for so long. Tell you what, let's order the sample kits for both programs and see what they are like this year. Then you can decide."

Mrs. Westphal seemed relieved and very comfortable with the idea.

A month went by and the night of the first vacation Bible school organizational meeting arrived. Mrs. Westphal had the two sample kits spread out on tables for everyone to see. She urged the teachers to take a look at them and then added, "I know we've always used Sonshine Soldiers before, but this year I kind of like Let the Children Come."

Inwardly Terry jumped for joy. The Lord had answered his prayers ("O, ye of little faith"). But he was totally unprepared for what Mrs. Westphal said next.

"It's very colorful and it really makes the Bible stories come alive."

It came as no surprise to Terry that the group agreed unanimously with Mrs. Westphal's assessment. After all, when it came to Christian education around here, she was "the chief." In giving Mrs. Westphal her proper due, Terry had managed to get her to come around to his way of thinking.

―――――

It takes wisdom, patience, tact, and perseverance to discover what church should look like for your small congregation and what the power structure you must operate in really is. Add a little dose of sanctified imagination, and you can use that knowledge to lead your people to be the best they can be.

You must keep a positive, optimistic attitude. If you're

convinced that the system stinks, the chieftains are incompetent, and God hasn't done anything in your congregation since 1955, then your church and your ministry will go nowhere.

Chapter 6 explains how you can feel good about your church by remembering what the church of Jesus Christ is really all about.

CHAPTER SIX

Looking for God in All the Wrong Places

"We are in an odd situation indeed when a Christian church is made to feel inadequate because the only reason it exists is for worship on Sunday."
—William H. Willimon and Robert L. Wilson[1]

"... it is absurd to try to judge the health and worth of a family by its size. We assess a family as it should be assessed: by the maturity of the individual members, the love they share together, the personal growth that they occasion for one another, by how well the next generation succeeds the first, and so on. Fortune 500 companies may want to judge their success on such criteria as percent increase of gross sales, percent of increase in profits, and so forth. These may be appropriate measures for corporate America, but they are not appropriate measures for judging our families. Why, then, do we in the church, especially the small church, feel a need to measure our success as if we were a corporation? In fact, we are a family, the very family of God."
—Anthony Pappas[2]

"Brothers, think of what you were when you were called. Not many of you were wise by human standards; not many were influential; not many were of noble birth. But God chose the foolish things of the world to shame the wise; God chose the weak things of the world to shame the strong ... so that no one may boast before him."
—1 Corinthians 1:26–27, 29

71

As Pastor Rutherford walked down the hall past the classroom door, he overheard the teacher telling her second-grade students the story of Noah and the flood. She was just to the part where God had decided to destroy mankind when suddenly a young voice shouted with a mixture of confusion and outrage, "What's he going to do that for?"

It was at that moment Pastor Rutherford realized that his small church had an excellent vacation Bible school program.

True, the classes were being held in the musty church basement—hardly the kind of environment that Baby Boomers were supposed to desire for their children. And several of the teachers and aides had never taught any kind of Bible class before. Some had even been recruited at the very last minute. The pastor didn't have a "well-qualified staff." His church couldn't even offer the full VBS program they had purchased because they didn't have anyone to act as a craft coordinator and didn't have any actors for the daily skit in the opening exercises.

And yet at vacation Bible school, children were being exposed to the Word of God. In fact, they were interacting with it. "After all," Pastor Rutherford thought, "isn't this what vacation Bible school is all about?"

Yes, that is what VBS should be all about. That's what the church is all about, for that matter. Sometimes, however, the church's true purpose is obscured by well-meaning Christians who emphasize other things. Churches are told that they must strive for "excellence"—excellence being defined as the ability to offer Baby Boomers and Generation Xers the same variety and quality of programs and services they've come to expect from corporate America.

We're told that individuals in these categories won't darken the door twice of any church that doesn't have a professionally printed bulletin. So the small congregation who has Mrs. Shaw as their secretary (good heart, but can't spell to save her life) and an antique Xerox machine down in a corner of the boiler room is out of luck when it comes to attracting new members. Boomers and Xers demand quality child care when they place their toddlers in the nursery. The small church who depends on second-hand toy donations and drafts whichever juniorhigh girl happens to show up on a Sunday morning as the nursery worker for the day will chase away any visitors they are lucky enough to get. People today are looking for a "seven-days-a-week church" and want many fellowship and support group options from which to choose. Poor little First Church who only offers Sunday school classes, a Wednesday night prayer group, and a once-a-month potluck supper should never hope to grow. The younger generation wants contemporary music in the worship service performed by talented professionals on first-class sound systems. This means that the small church has to kick old Mr. Green out of their choir (let's face it—he's tone deaf) and get rid of all those new hymnals that were donated last year by the Marini family in loving memory of Grandma Bernice.

Sacrifices will have to be made because the old, traditional forms of worship and the standard ways of doing church are definitely out. Now there are megachurches, metachurches, small-group movements, praise and worship leader training seminars, marketing strategies, and user-friendly, pre-evangelistic, entertainment-centered services. Proponents often tout these things as being God's blueprints for the twenty-first-century church. If your congregation isn't involved with one of the many new movements on the scene, then you are out of step with God.

The small church then, with their traditional mindset, limited financial resources, and scanty manpower base cannot hope to be a part of what God is doing today. God is with the Boomer and Xer congregations, helping them in their quest for "excellence." God blesses those who get with the program (and there are so many to choose from!). Real churches are those who not only serve quiche at their community suppers but also offer classes on how to make it. True churches subscribe to several church-growth newsletters, hire consultants, and add gymnasiums onto their sanctuaries. Small, "stuck in neutral" churches are only museum pieces—testimonies to the way God used to work in America. But we're entering the twenty-first century! God has gotten with it and you'd better, too, if you know what's good for you.[3]

Small-church leaders often get depressed and discouraged because they know full well that their congregations are never going to get with it. Many come to believe, therefore, that there's no chance their churches will ever see God's blessings. How could he bless a group who refuses to do what he wants them to do?

Here, however, is the main question: What does God want a church to do? How does a church obtain God's blessing? In my denomination, the Reformed Church in America, we believe that several historic documents accurately summarize the Bible's teachings. Two of these are the Heidelberg Catechism and the Belgic Confession. The Heidelberg Catechism says that the church is "a community chosen for eternal life and united in true faith" and that each member of that community receives gifts from Christ and has "a duty to use these gifts readily and cheerfully for the service and enrichment of the other members."[4] The Belgic Confession teaches that the true church preaches the Word, makes use of the sacraments, and practices discipline.[5] The Bible teaches that the church is Christ's body and exists to do his work and be a witness to his presence in the world.

Which of these biblical characteristics of the true church of Jesus Christ is missing in small, traditional congregations? None of them. What does the Bible say the church ought to do that a congregation with limited resources cannot do? Nothing. Whatever size your congregation, you can be true to the Bible's definition of a real, true, God-pleasing, God-blessed, purpose-fulfilling church. The way you carry out your mission will be different than the way the Boomer and Generation X churches carry out the same mission, but you can carry it out nonetheless.

Consider the parable of the talents in Matthew 25:14–30. Each servant was held accountable for making good use of the talents the master had given him. The servant with two talents invested them and when the master returned, the servant had two more to give him. This servant was commended, not chastised because he couldn't make more. God wants us to use what we have, not moan about what we don't have. The megachurch may be able to return five more talents to the Master. You may only be able to return one or two. The parable makes it clear that God wants that one or two and will be well pleased with them. The only way a church can incur the Master's wrath is by refusing to use the resources God has given them. God will not hold you accountable to match the deeds and ministries of a larger church. You will be accountable, however, to be the best small church you can possibly be.

Leaders in small churches don't have to feel doomed from the start—unable to do the Lord's will. Instead, they should lift up their eyes for the fields are white unto harvest. There are many ways for even the smallest congregation to be true to the church's calling.

The pastor looked again at the huge, unopened mailer on her desk. It was from the denomination's office for social ministry.

"Well," she sighed, "it's finally here. Yet another thing to make me feel guilty."

She had known the denomination was making a big push this year to get congregations involved in social outreach—

"A Cup of Cold Water for Christ" the campaign was called. She knew what would be in the packet even before she opened it. She would read glowing testimonies about congregations who had started soup kitchens, shelters for the homeless, neighborhood clean-up campaigns, and crisis pregnancy centers. There would be guidebooks to show how her congregation could "go and do thou likewise." And there would be forms for ordering materials that would educate her congregation about the tasks at hand. Such materials were being made available at a minimal cost to every church in the denomination.

But that was the problem, wasn't it? Her congregation couldn't even afford to pay a minimal cost. They were barely able to pay her a salary. And the last new program she had tried to organize in the church never got past the board. If anything was proposed that the church hadn't already been doing for the last twenty years, it was quickly voted down. Besides, there were many in the congregation who viewed social witness as something "liberals" were preoccupied with. True churches spent their time preaching the Good News.

So once again, the pastor would let down her denomination and, more importantly, God. Once again, she was being called to lead her congregation into an area they couldn't or wouldn't go into.

As she threw her head back to release some of the tension building up in her neck and shoulders, her eyes happened to fall on the calendar hanging on the office wall. In two more weeks the church was having their autumn rummage sale. Twice a year, autumn and spring, the church collected used clothing, dishes, toys, books, and appliances from the congregation and the surrounding neighborhoods and held a sale. Proceeds went to help meet the church's budget.

The pastor's heart brightened. Hadn't she seen the faces of poor people light up when they entered the fellowship hall with its table upon table of inexpensive but essential wares?

Hadn't she been told that people living at or near the poverty level looked forward to the semiannual events? Didn't the church usually have a pickup truck load or two of goods left over that they donated to nearby inner-city missions?

She cast her mind forward to the Advent season. Every year the Sunday school department baked dozens and dozens of Christmas cookies and took them to a food pantry run by one of the bigger churches in the area. There the cookies were distributed to the poor.

The pastor thought about the springtime. Last May, a family in the community lost their home in a fire. The church took up a special collection for them, provided them with some home-cooked meals, and contributed some items that were immediately essential (clothing, toiletries, etc.).

The pastor smiled. Maybe her small flock wasn't participating in the "A Cup of Cold Water for Christ" program, but they were offering drinks to the needy just the same. The small church may not have been involved in social outreach at the same level of intensity and commitment as larger congregations, but tangible acts of love and kindness were being done in Christ's name. Suddenly, the pastor didn't feel so bad about her people.

She even opened the packet. "Who knows?" she thought. "Maybe there will be a suggestion for a project in here that's right up our alley."

———

A mini-revolt was brewing among the younger children in the church. Why, they wanted to know, was there a youth fellowship for the junior and senior high school students, but nothing comparable for them? Their good question received the same old small-church answers.

— "We've never had anything like it before. Nobody would know what to do."

— "Who's got the time to run such a program?"

— "There's no money in the budget for it."

However, a group of parents in the congregation got together and decided it couldn't be that hard to do. True, their time was precious. They already wore many hats in the small congregation. But couldn't they give up one hour, one Saturday morning a month to give the children a youth group? And couldn't it be done without any real cost to the church?

One of the mothers who was musically gifted said she could open each meeting with twenty minutes of Christian songs and choruses that lent themselves to physical motions and interpretative dance. Another mother said she'd be willing to come up with twenty minutes of games using supplies she had on hand at home (milk cartons, string, balls, etc.). A father who was a ham at heart came up with the idea of reading a story to the children and then helping them act it out for the last twenty minutes. He would use the Bible and Christian children's books that his family had lying around the house. A couple of times a year, the group would have a special activity—a sledding party, a picnic, or a game night—requiring very little advance preparation or funds.

After the group started, the church would receive ads in the mail for prepackaged youth programs, all requiring more workers and money than the congregation had. But it didn't matter. A successful program was already in place, a program that let children know they were important to the Lord and the Lord's people.

———■———

God can and does use modest ideas as well as grandiose dreams. God can and does speak in the gentle whisper as well as in the wind, earthquake, and fire. The Lord can use the small church's traditional Christmas pageant as well as the professional dramatists and musicians at Willow Creek.

If you're a Willow Creek-minded leader serving in a small church, you don't necessarily have to give up your dreams. But you do have to be patient and learn how to rejoice over whatever progress is being made.

We wouldn't expect a missionary going to an Islamic country to be able to establish a megachurch in five years. He or she is laboring in a culture that is hostile to the Gospel. Instead after the missionary has been in the field a year, we rejoice when he or she reports that two or three people have expressed interest in learning more about Jesus and a group of six Christians meet once every two weeks for a "secret" time of Bible study and prayer. We recognize God has called that missionary to labor in a hard field that has been closed to the church for centuries. Any step forward, however small, is a step in the right direction. We gratefully praise the Lord for each and every "baby step" in much the same way young parents get excited when their child first starts to walk.

Leaders in the church growth movement admit that small, established, traditional churches are often hostile to their ideas. Growth-minded pastors are told that their ministry in these congregations will be a lot like trying to pump water uphill—"It can be done, but it means opposing the forces of nature and requires persistent and continuous effort."[6] Small churches have remained tradition-bound and closed to change for years. Shouldn't leaders rejoice, then, when congregations take even small steps forward? Perhaps your worship service isn't yet "seeker sensitive," but have you at least persuaded the board to start printing the page numbers for the doxology, the Apostles' Creed, the Lord's Prayer, the responsive reading, the Scripture lesson, and the Gloria Patri in the bulletin? Maybe your congregation has not yet formed cell groups, but have you been able to start a men's prayer breakfast? You may not have a praise and worship team yet, but once in awhile are you able to incorporate some contemporary music in the Sunday morning service?

Small-church leaders should be excited and encouraged whenever they see their congregations begin to hesitantly toddle forward, instead of becoming depressed because "junior" isn't yet ready to join the track and field team. To be blunt, the sins of impatience, jealousy, discontent, and walking by sight instead of by faith are behind some of the frustrations that small-church leaders experience. We want what other congregations have and we want it *now!* We wonder why God had to saddle us with this bunch of losers. How much more effective we could be if only we were in a larger church! Our congregations don't make the denominational executives or the national news magazines sit up and take notice, therefore God doesn't notice us either. Because we don't see dramatic results from our work, we assume that God isn't doing much of anything through us.

If only we could truly see things from God's perspective and realize that small congregations have what it takes when it comes to fulfilling his desires for the church. We need to be more like proud parents and less like carping critics when it comes to our congregations. And just as parents find ways to encourage babies to take more small steps ("Walk to Grandma! You can do it! Go get the ball! Go get the ball!") small-church leaders need to find ways to encourage their congregations to take even tiny steps forward in their walk as the Lord's people.

The next two chapters deal with ways to do just that.

CHAPTER SEVEN

Show Them the Termites

"And then ... Og gonna die!"
—the signature line of the cartoon character Og in the television program, *Cro*

"Problems once registered may be dealt with by ignoring them. This is not an uncommon small church response and sometimes a viable one!"
—Anthony G. Pappas[1]

There's a (probably apocryphal) story told of one pastor's frustration in trying to get his congregation to do something about their building's infestation of termites. At the first board meeting about the problem, the members discussed what sort of pesticide should be used to get rid of the insects. Farmer Goode shared the name of the stuff he had used in his barn. Immediately Kate Vaughn (the church's self-appointed environmentalist) spoke up, insisting that the chemical was dangerous and the only way it would be sprayed in the church would be over her dead body. No action on the problem was taken.

At the next meeting, it was suggested that an exterminator be called in. But which exterminator? Should the board go with one of the branch outfits of a national chain or with a friend of Ed's who worked as a janitor for the school and did this sort of thing on the side? Several members shifted uncomfortably in their seats. Seems they weren't too happy with the job another friend of Ed's did when he painted the storage shed. "He wasn't just my friend," Ed snarled, "he was my son-in-law. That shed was painted a year ago. How come I'm just hearing about your complaints now? That's the trouble with

81

this church, there's entirely too much dishonesty, backbiting, and complaining!" This led to a long discussion about the spiritual state of the church in general, and Ed and the critics of his son-in-law in particular. No action was taken on the termites.

At the third meeting, concern was expressed over whether or not the church could afford to pay a professional to do the job. Couldn't we just do it ourselves? It'd be cheaper. One of the elders spoke out demanding to know why God's people had to go second-class. The answer, he was told, was that God's people weren't living up to their biblical responsibility to tithe. The church's real trouble was that they never ran any stewardship campaigns. Speeches were then heard, pro and con, on the merits of running such a campaign next fall. The termites were all but forgotten.

Finally, at the fourth meeting, the pastor whipped out a glass jar in which he had placed a few of the insects and some pieces of wood. Placing the jar in the center of the table he said, "Ladies and gentlemen, these are termites. Our building is full of them. See what they're doing to that wood? That's what they're doing to our sanctuary, even to the floor underneath our feet, as we are sitting here. Now, what are we going to do about it?"

Within five minutes the board had decided on an exterminator, decided to give him free license to use whatever chemicals he felt appropriate, and decided to pay him by taking up a special emergency collection.

This story illustrates four very important principles that any small-church leader must keep in mind if he or she is going to get the congregation to take any kind of action.

1. *A small-church leader is primarily a problem presenter, not a problem solver.* A mistake that many pastors make is to assume that small churches are hiring them as "outside experts" who are to come into the congregation and fix what's wrong. Actually, small churches hire pastors to be well-

informed committee members who can help *their groups* come to consensus decisions on problems and challenges. Put another way, a pastor (or any leader) is seen as one of the family who has been called to a family conference. He or she isn't supposed to arrive at the meeting with prepackaged, ready-made answers. Instead, the pastor is supposed to work with the family to find solutions that seem reasonable to everyone. Family members don't want pronouncements handed down from patriarchs or matriarchs. They want a family conference that is truly a conference. They want to be part of the process, not just called on to rubber-stamp a conclusion. Leaders who don't understand this come to board meetings armed with ten-page proposals, charts and graphs, and answers to any and all conceivable objections only to have their ideas dismissed in short order. The effective small-church leader soon discovers his or her job is to clearly define existing problems and seek the group's input on how to solve them.[2]

In the termite story, would action have been taken so quickly at the fourth meeting if everyone had not been previously able to express their opinions on the subject (and everything remotely related to it)? Would the group have gone along with the pastor saying at the first meeting, "We've got a termite problem, so I looked up Rid-Ex in the phone book, and they're willing to come by next Wednesday and take care of the little pests for $350. All in favor say, 'aye'"?

Of course action was finally taken, due in a large degree to the pastor's clever presentation of the problem. This leads us to the second principle.

2. *Leaders should present problems in as graphic and as personal a manner as possible.* In the cartoon show *Cro*, the caveman Og always fixates on his problems, extrapolating all the terrible things he's sure are going to happen to him and ending his reverie by screaming in panic that he's going to die. Small-church leaders need to be like Og, not in always

believing the church is about to end and thereby exhibiting little or no faith in God, but by using their imaginations to project all the consequences that could result if a problem isn't solved soon.

The reason problems must be presented in as serious a light as possible is because small-church members who cling to their traditions will never make any changes unless they are forced to do so. Anthony Pappas writes, ". . . an accident is always more motivational in a folk society than an argument." He quotes John A. Hostetler as saying, "When taken as 'acts of God,' new courses of action, which would otherwise be resented, are made legitimate." Pappas urges small-church leaders to "let life provide the impetus to faithfulness."[3]

The pastor in the story did that by making the board members feel as though the very floor they were sitting on was about to give way.

3. *It takes time for small congregations to decide to take action.* Often it will take awhile to reach a crisis point where there is no alternative but to take action. Congregations will wait for that point. Everybody knows something needs to be done about that old dead tree near the parking lot, but nobody moves to chop it down until limbs begin falling around the board members' cars.

Small-church people will not accept ideas that come in from the outside. They need to feel that the ideas are theirs, generated from within the family. If a person hears about a new plan often enough over a long period of time, chances are they will begin to be more open to it. It becomes familiar, not threatening. In fact, the person may begin to believe that parts of the plan were his or her idea to being with!

Finally, boards can get so sick of discussing the same subject over and over again at every meeting, they will take action just to remove it from the agenda.

The bottom line for the small-church leader is not to get too discouraged when nothing seems to be happening. The idea may just be taking awhile to simmer. The crisis may need time to come to a boil. The plan may even now be slowly permeating the hearts and minds of the congregation. A good leader prays for and cultivates patience. He or she makes sure everyone gets a chance to have a say and isn't afraid to table business until the next meeting, giving everyone a chance to pray about it and sleep on it. It took four meetings before the termites were dealt with, but they were dealt with.

4. *A leader must help his or her people remove obstacles that prevent them from seeing the problem clearly.* How much clearer could the termite problem have been presented than to have a jar full of the little monsters right in front of everyone's face? But even before that, the seemingly off-track, disruptive discussions at the previous board meetings were actually clearing the air and allowing members to get things off their chests so they would be able to concentrate on the problem at hand. Kate was able to say her piece about the environment. Ed was able to express his concern over the way members dealt with each other. The hot topic of tithing was discussed. A wise leader realizes that people sometimes have so much baggage piled up in front of them that they can see nothing else. He or she will allow them time to remove the pile before pressing for a decision.

A leader recognizes that people carry around not only political and theological baggage, but also very personal baggage. Elder Riley is having problems with a rebellious teenage son. The night before the board meeting, they had an argument that shook the house. When Riley arrives at the board meeting, he's likely to be in an irritable mood. After all, he was up all night sick with worry, guilt, and confusion. He'll be easily distracted. His mind won't be on any of the business at hand. In fact, it will all seem very trivial and petty to him. Deacon Tammy Krebs is being harassed by her boss at work.

He is a chauvinistic pig who gives all the plum assignments to the males and leaves her to do the "drudge jobs." He shoots down any idea she has. Now it's board meeting night, is it? Well, Tammy knows one thing for sure—no male member had better question her proposal for splitting the youth group into two separate age brackets or she'll hand him his head. She may have to put up with that junk at work, but no way is she putting up with it at church on her own time!

Good leaders know that board and committee members have a life outside the church and that life receives ninety-six percent of the members' attention. The leader must acknowledge that life and help the members deal with it before they will be ready to turn their attention to the concerns of the church. This can be done by building a time of prayer for one another's requests into each meeting's agenda. It can be accomplished by going up to Elder Riley before the meeting and saying, "You look very tired tonight. Is everything all right?" A lunch can be scheduled with Deacon Tammy just so "We can have a chance to chat. I've heard that things have been really awful at your job lately." When members know there will be definite opportunities to deal with their personal problems later, they find it much easier to shelve those problems and concentrate on the business at hand. When they are reminded that the other members are not enemies but people who genuinely care for them, their blood pressures back away from the boiling point.

Leaders who consciously or unconsciously follow these four principles are able to move their small churches to take action, make changes, and solve problems.

───────

The sound system in the sanctuary was antiquated and in disrepair. It had been cobbled together by do-it-yourselfers out of pieces of old stereos about twenty years ago. Now one of the speakers cut in and out, and the monitor in the nursery was dead. Tape recordings of the service couldn't be done on the system. Instead, a small, hand-held recorder was placed at the back of the church.

The new pastor asked several board members if there was any chance the system could be upgraded. They each laughed and said, "Well, we've discussed it at three or four meetings every year for the last five years and nothing's happened yet. Don't worry about it. Somebody will get around to doing something about it someday. It's kind of a low priority compared with other things we need to deal with."

Yet within the year, the church had a brand-new, professionally installed sound system. What happened?

The pastor began asking the shut-ins if they made use of the tapes he brought them. They sheepishly admitted that they rarely tried to listen to them anymore because it was next to impossible to hear and understand anything the pastor or anyone else was saying. The pastor and the elder who aided with visitation reported to the board at their next meeting that the church wasn't fulfilling their duty to minister to the spiritual lives of their shut-ins. The pastor and elder explained why. Another person spoke up. "We're not just letting our shut-ins down, we're letting our visitors down as well," he said. "Last Sunday I invited my grandfather to the worship service, and while he thought the people were very nice and friendly, he confessed to me that he hadn't been able to hear a thing!" A brief discussion took place with the conclusion, "We really need to get moving on that sound system."

Later in the meeting, a different concern was raised. The pastor shared that several key families in the congregation were upset because the church had a large sum of money in the bank that was "just sitting there and not being used for the Lord's work." The board members moaned. They had been through all this before when they had decided to invest the money instead of putting it into the general fund. "I'm sick of those people grousing. Somebody should just tell them to shut up!" one elder growled. A deacon offered a suggestion. "Can't we find a way to appease them, to show them that we're not the money-hoarders they think we are? Maybe we could find a mission project to support or something in the church that really needs to be done and use just a portion of the money to do it. That way we would show them that we don't save money at the expense of ministry, and we still will have an investment like we originally wanted."

No decision on the matter was arrived at that evening, but the phone lines were buzzing over the next few weeks and many informal, unofficial, "mini-board meetings" were held. At the next official meeting, a motion was carried to hire audio experts to install a new sound system as soon as possible using a portion of the invested money.

Take a moment to go back and review the stories of Cathy Gordon and Pastor Johnson from Chapter 1 and the Sunday school superintendent in Chapter 2. Could their stories have turned out differently?

What if Cathy Gordon had engaged the whole ladies fellowship in a discussion of what might be done to increase attendance? What if she had offered as a suggestion contacting the denomination to see if they could help? What if she let one of the other women place the phone call? What if each woman talked to one of the younger women to find out why she wasn't coming and what, if anything, could be done to encourage her to become involved?

What if Pastor Johnson had told his board that he had spoken to both the new choir director and Ralph and found that, although they both were sincere Christians, they had very different opinions about what constituted proper music for the worship service? What if he asked the board how a compromise could be worked out, saying that the church certainly didn't want to lose Ralph or the director? What if he expressed concern over the way Ralph voiced his complaints and then suggested that people in the church needed to have a means of expressing their feelings to the board—could a suggestion box be put in the lobby, or one or two elders designated as a complaint compartment? Should Pastor Johnson preach and teach more on how to handle disputes in the church? And what if Pastor Johnson pleaded with Ralph to agree to disagree in love with the director, volunteering to go with him to help patch up the relationship?[4]

What if the Sunday school superintendent, instead of jumping in with a solution, had just empathized with the teachers saying, "I know that children in those age brackets are tough to reach. Even if they like what you're doing, it's not 'cool' for them to let you know. They can be into a lesson one week and act like they could care less what you're talking about the next. It's not always easy and rewarding to deal with them. Let's spend some time at the end of the meeting praying that God would give you wisdom and the ability to persevere, not to mention that he'd open the hearts of the students. And some of you who have experience dealing with kids that age, make sure you talk to the teachers and give them some suggestions that have worked for you." Many a leader has found that when individuals vent their spleen about how badly things are going in the church, they are really just saying that they have been having a hard time lately and are feeling unloved and unsupported. After they are offered a sympathetic shoulder to cry on and an empathetic ear to listen to their woes, they suddenly find things in the church aren't so bad after all. The program doesn't need to be dropped or changed. They don't have to resign. The condition is improving.

Of course there is no guarantee that if Cathy, Pastor Johnson, and the superintendent had recognized the four principles and based their actions upon those and other insights offered in this book that their stories would have had happier endings. As was pointed out in Chapter 2, people and groups can be irrational, emotional, and completely unpredictable at times. However, leaders have a better chance for happier endings if they follow the four principles than if they don't. As a leader, don't you want to do everything you can to increase the chances for success?

What about the stories in Chapters 1 and 2 of people who became frustrated when they tried to get their small churches to grow? How can one move insular, tradition-bound groups to reach out in the name of Christ? We will turn our attention to this question in the next chapter.

CHAPTER EIGHT

From No Growth to Pro-Growth

"All authority in heaven and on earth has been given to me. Therefore go and make disciples of all nations...."
—Jesus Christ (Matthew 28:18–19)

"And the Lord added to their number daily those who were being saved."
—Acts 2:47

"The outsider is an enemy almost by definition."
—Anthony Pappas[1]

"In the small church there are no strangers. Everyone knows everyone else. The social situation is predictable and therefore comfortable. Preserving this value by maintaining the status quo becomes a very high priority in the lives of many church members."
—C. Peter Wagner[2]

The small church has a bad reputation for being "against growth" because it balks at plans coming out of the church-growth movement. But smaller congregations have been unfairly labeled. It's not that they are against growth; it's that they are against changing the characteristics that make them unique.[3] Small congregations aren't opposed to bringing men and women to Christ, but they are opposed to becoming megachurches. They don't want to be asked to become something they are not. Unfortunately, some evangelism

programs ask small churches to do just that. The congregation rebels at the idea, and the leader becomes discouraged
because his or her people "won't do anything to help the
church grow."

Actually, small churches can work for growth as long as
they are first assured that the resulting congregations will still
have a small-church flavor.[4]

Members in small congregations fear strangers.

— "Strangers don't understand our history, our traditions,
   the way we do things around here. Things that are
   important to us won't necessarily be important to them.
   And we like going to a church where we know everyone else."
— "It feels like home. Sunday morning is a family
   reunion. If too many strangers start showing up, the
   intimate atmosphere will evaporate. It sure won't seem
   like our church anymore."

The surest way to overcome a small congregation's fear of
strangers is to make sure none get invited to the worship service. Assure your people that you see your church's mission
not as reaching out to the young families or single mothers in
your community, but to the friends, neighbors, coworkers,
and relatives of your members. Therefore, new members
won't be strangers but folks already known and loved.

The first step in reaching out to your "target group" is to
poll the congregation to find out what would get people they
know to "darken the door" of the church. What aspects of life
do friends need help with? What about God and "religion"
puzzles them? Plan sermon series, Bible studies, and seminars on these topics.

━━━

One small church has seen numerical growth through a com-
bination of "invite-a-friend Sundays" and nonthreatening

social events. Twice a year, members are encouraged to bring friends and relatives to a special Sunday worship service that celebrates friendship. The sermons have centered on such themes as "Jesus, the Friend of Sinners" and "Abraham, God's Friend." The Gospel is always communicated in a clear, but nonthreatening way (i.e., no altar calls or raising of hands with "every eye closed, every head bowed"). After the service, a "coffee hour in honor of our friends" is held in the fellowship hall with baked goodies a plenty. Later in the week, a letter from the pastor goes out to all visitors thanking them for helping to make Sunday special and inviting them to come again some time.

Once every quarter, the church hosts "family fun night" (talent shows, picnics, ethnic food festivals, etc.). Members are encouraged to use these events to introduce friends and family to people in the congregation in a "nonreligious" setting. Friends have come for something to do on a Saturday night, to see what act the kids cooked up, or to sample some free food and have ended up becoming regular attenders of Sunday morning worship. People outside a local church are afraid of strangers, too. They aren't anxious to come out and be mobbed by small-church members as "our visitor this Sunday." Anything the local church can do to "break the ice" and introduce potential Sunday visitors to the congregation beforehand will reap dividends later.

━━━■━━━

Social events like family fun night go a long way towards reducing a congregation's fear of losing intimacy as it starts to add new members. Nothing, however, alleviates that fear more than assurances from the leaders that they will not sacrifice the close-knit, family feel of a small church on the altar of growth.

━━━■━━━

Pastor Kim's small congregation had enthusiastically embraced all her plans and goals for church growth, and as a result, the sanctuary was now almost full on Sunday mornings. But instead of rejoicing over this harvest of souls for Christ, board members were making statements like these:

— "It's getting so there's no place to park anymore."
— "I couldn't name half the people in our church if I had to."
— "I don't know how to tell the visitors and members apart."
— "I can't put my finger on it, but something isn't right about the way things are going lately."

The board began balking at Kim's latest proposals. So she called a special meeting and addressed the issue head-on.

"I praise the Lord that we've been growing quickly," she said, "but it could be that we haven't yet properly dealt with the consequences of our growth. I don't want the people attending Sunday morning to feel that they are in a building full of strangers. If we grow much bigger, I think we may have to go to two worship services. Also, I need your ideas about starting some home fellowship groups. You see, no matter how large we grow, I want every member to be among friends on Sunday morning and to have a close circle of Christian brothers and sisters to fellowship with and to turn to in times of trouble. I need your help so that in our quest for growth, we don't throw away the very things that make our congregation so special and attractive in the first place."

"You've got our help, Pastor," the board pledged.

Once again they began approving Kim's ideas and adopting her goals. She had shown that she understood them and, at heart, was one of them.

Closely linked with the fear of strangers and the fear of losing intimacy is the fear of losing control, of seeing the church mutate into something alien and undesirable, yet being unable to stop it. New members will bring new ideas. More numbers added to the roll means an upset in the balance of power. There may come a day when the relative newcomers outnumber the old-timers, those who have given years of blood, sweat, and tears to ensure the church's survival. And what if the newcomers are able to outvote the long-term members?

—"What if they force their will down our throats?"
—"What if they, inexperienced as they are, make a ship-wreck of this congregation that we've given our lives to?"

Fear can be lessened by making sure that both established and new members have a voice in how the church is run. Committees and boards should have representatives from both groups serving on them. And once again, leaders must assure the congregation that they have no intention to grow at the expense of the existing members.[5]

Another problem Pastor Kim's church faced is very common to growing American churches in the 1990s. What should the worship service look like? Younger people were asking for more contemporary music. Some members who came from a more Pentecostal background or who were participating in the charismatic renewal movement wanted Sunday mornings to be "free in the Spirit." Yet some vocal, long-term members wanted Sunday mornings to be the same as they had always been, proceeding according to the established liturgy.

At that same special board meeting, Pastor Kim told the gathering that she desired to find a format for the worship service that, if not able to totally please everybody, would at least be something everyone would feel comfortable with. All would feel as though they were able to "really worship" God when the congregation came together on Sundays. Board members decided to informally "poll" church members to determine what styles and elements of worship they felt were most meaningful. Then, at a regularly scheduled meeting, the board would list the things mentioned and see if it was possible to structure a worship service that would meet everyone's spiritual needs.

The service they came up with adhered very closely to the traditional liturgy except that the first hymn was replaced by ten minutes of praise and worship music, and a time for testimonies and sharing prayer requests was included right after the announcements. The new format seemed to satisfy the younger members, at least for the time being. The older members saw that they could welcome new people and even embrace a few new ideas without having to scrap all they held dear. Young members felt free to keep inviting their friends. Older members kept giving visitors a warm welcome. The church kept growing.

Fear of failure, disappointment, and frustration also stop many small congregations from attempting to grow. A congregation that has remained plateaued at a certain number of members for many years begins to believe this number is the norm.

— "We're never going to get any bigger, so why try?"
— "Obviously, the church is at just the right size in God's eyes, or else he would have caused us to grow."
— "Outreach programs are doomed to fail because they attempt to tamper with the natural order of things. First Church has between fifty and seventy-five members—that's the way we're always going to be."

And yet many churches who are now plateaued didn't use to be. Small congregations can often look back to a "golden age"—the long ago "glory days" under beloved Pastor Clark Kent when the sanctuary was filled to the rafters. A wise leader will act as a historian and remind the church of what they once were while challenging them to be like that again. The small congregation needs to see that the way things are now is not necessarily the norm for the church. One pastor helped his small church begin a youth program not by exhorting the people to do all they could to win needy teens to Christ but by reminding them how much youth fellowship meant to them as they were growing up. Can't we give our kids this wonderful experience, too?

However, sometimes a leader's backward pointing can have a negative effect when people are reminded of evangelism programs in the past that failed miserably. Who wants to go through all that again? If the leader can't find a successful idea from the church's past to recycle and retool for today, he or she is better off suggesting plans that are as different as possible from what the church tried in the past. If your congregation relied heavily on advertising in the past, why not concentrate on "invitation only" events? If the only thing the church has ever invited the community to is Sunday morning worship, why not sponsor a marriage seminar? If the community won't come to the church, why not take the church to the community via free car washes, park clean-ups, etc.?

Plans should be implemented that have as little chance for "failure" as possible. For example, "invite-a-friend Sunday" comes to mind. One congregation tried it and had only four visitors that morning. None of the four came back again or joined the church, but the congregation didn't feel it was all "for nothing." At least four friends heard the Gospel, had a great time visiting with the church members during coffee hour, and left feeling that Faith Presbyterian wasn't such a bad place after all. What's wrong with that? When you plan programs and campaigns, make sure that the worst that can happen really isn't very bad.

Once in awhile when board members turn down evangelism proposals, what they are really saying is, "I'm tired." In any church, it always seems as though twenty percent of the people do eighty percent of the work. In the small church that twenty percent can be five to twenty individuals, most of whom probably serve on the board. When they hear of a new idea, all they can think of is, "How in the world am I going to find time for that?" If a leader can go to the board with not only an outreach proposal but also the names of people who are willing to work on it, the chances of that proposal winning approval will dramatically increase. One pastor was able to get his board to go along with a plan that required door-to-door visitation, even though the board members had tried something similar years before. He did it by assuring them that they wouldn't have to be involved. Workers were already lined up.

Now comes the part of this chapter which I dread writing and you may dread reading because it may sound as if I'm picking on you. That's not my intention. But it is my intention to state the truth, and the truth is that some small churches won't grow because they are outside the will of God. Nancy Clark, a small-church expert in my denomination, said about one small congregation that needed to grow, "Before, or parallel to numerical growth, spiritual and emotional growth needed to be fostered."[6]

If the members of a congregation don't understand the message of the Bible—that friends and neighbors are lost without Christ—they won't be motivated to reach out. If a church is not a place where people feel they are encountering God and having their lives touched and enriched in places the world cannot reach, then the church isn't going to be able to offer much to outsiders. A person can find a sense of community and worthwhile projects to do by joining the

Rotary Club or the PTA. He or she doesn't have to join an organization that requires their members to get up early and assemble every Sunday morning. If your church offers nothing more than secular organizations offer (organizations which usually have more resources and often better facilities), then you needn't wonder why you aren't growing.

Also, if members of your congregation are feuding with each other, visitors to the worship service won't want to come back. In a small church, it's hard to hide the fact that several people aren't on speaking terms. It's obvious, too, if the rest of the congregation is avoiding a person or persons. Sometimes the atmosphere of tension in a small church is so thick you can cut it with a knife. Outsiders pick up that if they were to join the congregation, they would be asked to choose sides in a war or wars. Instead, they choose another church.

Leaders in small churches who are working to bring their groups to a higher level of spiritual or emotional maturity shouldn't despair that they aren't "doing much of anything for growth." Pastors who prepare relevant, biblical sermons and studies in order to deepen their congregations' understanding of God, themselves, and their places in God's plan are "church-growth pastors" even if they haven't gotten around yet to doing demographic studies of their areas. Leaders who spend time playing the role of peacemaker are working for numerical growth even though they haven't been handing out tracts in front of the supermarket (besides—Jesus says they are blessed!).

Organisms will only prosper in healthy environments that are conducive to growth. The healthiest environment for the church is love. Love begins with the leaders. Chapter 9 deals with how the leader can love his or her people.

CHAPTER NINE

The Gospel in a Word Is Love

"I always thank God for you because of his grace given you in Christ Jesus. For in him you have been enriched in every way—in all your speaking and in all your knowledge—because our testimony about Christ was confirmed in you. Therefore you do not lack any spiritual gift as you eagerly wait for our Lord Jesus Christ to be revealed."

—The apostle Paul to a church riddled with serious problems in 1 Corinthians 1:4–7

"If anyone says, 'I love God,' yet hates his brother, he is a liar. For anyone who does not love his brother, whom he has seen, cannot love God, whom he has not seen. And he has given us this command: Whoever loves God must also love his brother."

—1 John 4:20–21

Getting a little punchy from writing one day, I decided to play a joke on my wife. I announced that I was going into my study to do some more work, then emerged ten minutes later with a few sheets of scrap paper stapled together on which I'd produced a comic book drawn and written in the style used by my eight-year-old son. I excitedly rushed over to my wife announcing, "My book is done! It's finished!"

As she read it, she commented, "This really says a lot, you know."

"Oh, come on. It's a joke!" I laughed.

"No, I mean it. Take another look at it. Doesn't it sum up the attitudes of too many pastors today?"

I had to admit that she was right. If a member of a small

church could be a fly on the wall at a gathering of pastors, he
or she may be quite shocked to hear the way many pastors

talk about their congregations.[1] Pastors complain that their people are burdens, not blessings—always calling them to gripe and complain or involve them in petty problems, while not doing much to advance the kingdom of God. Pastors wonder why God placed them in small churches. Surely with their gifts and abilities, they could do more for the cause of Christ if they were pastoring larger, "more active" congregations. Pastors talk about the need to whip their people into shape—to get those lazy sinners off their butts and get them moving for the Lord. Pastors could always get more done if only those stupid, stubborn, old-fashioned board members wouldn't keep putting on the brakes. And more than one pastor has made a shambles of one small church after another as they attempt to "lead, direct, exhort, and correct" (read "bully") congregations into doing "the Lord's will."

It bothers me when I hear pastors talking this way (however I must confess I've made one or two comments along these lines myself) because our words reflect the state of our hearts (Matthew 15:18; Luke 6:45). Leaders may feel justified in complaining about the sorry state of their people, but what about the sorry state of their own hearts? Okay, maybe your congregation is sinning by not doing all they could to obey the Great Commission. Maybe certain cliques in your church ignore God's commands for peace and unity. Maybe you are trying to minister to a congregation of blatantly unrepentant sinners. Does that give you the right to sin, too?[2] The same God who commands you to boldly proclaim his word also commands you to love his people. First John 4:21 says, "Whoever loves God must also love his brother." Except if his brother is immature? Except if his brother is a pest? Except if his brother stands in the way of important things that really need to get done? Except if his brother is still an imperfect sinner? No, love your brother, period.

Not only is love commanded in the Bible, it is also the channel of change in the small church. As was stated earlier in this book, people in small congregations will not accept your leadership until you become "one of the gang." It's awfully hard to become one of the gang if you secretly despise the members of the gang. A study of the apostle Paul's letters will reveal that a number of times he used the love he had for his congregations and the mutual love they had for him as a basis for asking the churches to accept his authority, believe his doctrine, follow his example, and take action as he directed (1 Corinthians 4:14–15; 2 Corinthians 1:23–24; 6:11–13; Galatians 4:12–16, 19; Philippians 1:7–8, 16; 2:1–2; 4:1; 1 Thessalonians 2:7–12; Philemon 8–11, 19–20). Paul understood, as John Maxwell says, "People don't care how much you know until they know how much you care."[3]

It's often hard for pastors in small churches to really care for their people. First John 4:18 teaches that, ". . . perfect love drives out fear, because fear has to do with punishment. The one who fears is not made perfect in love." Fear also casts out love. Many pastors can't love their congregations because they fear their congregations and what they believe their churches could do to them.[4]

In a small church the pastor knows everyone. If a family becomes discouraged with the church's ministry and leaves, the pastor feels the hurt of losing a friend. What's more, everyone in the congregation will notice that the Smiths are gone and wonder what the trouble is. Could it be . . . *the pastor's fault?!!*

The pastor's job in the small church is often hanging by a thread. Because every individual's opinions and complaints are taken seriously, the pastor knows that if he or she upsets even a couple of people, the whole church may soon be clamoring to see a resignation. And the financial base of the church is so small that if a family leaves, the congregation suddenly won't be able to pay the pastor's salary.

The pastor believes that if he or she should have to leave, he or she would have a very difficult time being called to a "good church." After all, the pastor can't show many "great victories" on his or her résumé. Not that there weren't opportunities for victories at the current church, but the congregation refused to go along with what needed to be done. The pastor sees his or her people standing in the way of the pastor's career advancement and "dooming" him or her to a life of serving one tiny church after another.

Even if members in the congregation aren't presently threatening the pastor's financial livelihood, they can threaten his or her physical, mental, emotional, and spiritual stability. The small-church pastor often doesn't have a secretary to screen phone calls, established office hours after which he or she is considered to be "off duty," or the luxury of cutting off one of Mrs. Jones' three-hour conversations by saying, "I'm really busy today." Mrs. Jones and the rest of the congregation believe that it's the pastor's job to spend endless hours on the phone listening to their problems and concerns. The pastor is the center of the small church's universe, the hub around which everything revolves. It is automatically assumed that the pastor must be part of, or at least informed about, every bit of ministry that the congregation does—from choir practice to committee meetings to one member calling on another who is sick. I have visited in several pastor's homes where the phone rang every ten to fifteen minutes. The poor men couldn't relax, spend time with their families, or even eat their dinners! Too many nights like this and the pastor and his or her family will begin to go nuts.

Is it any wonder then that some pastors begin to view their congregations as enemies rather than friends? If the pastor is to love and not loathe his or her congregation, the pastor must overcome his or her fear of being hurt by the people. How? Let's turn our attention again to Paul.

The same apostle who daily faced the pressure of his concern for his beloved churches (2 Corinthians 11:28) was also able to distance himself from them when he needed to. Paul did not question his authority or effectiveness as an apostle just because the churches in Galatia and Corinth were going down the tubes. He knew what God had called him to do and was confident that he had been faithful. After warning Timothy that "evil men and impostors will go from bad to worse" (2 Timothy 3:13) and exhorting him to keep his head in performing all the duties of his ministry (2 Timothy 4:5), he says, "I have fought the good fight, I have finished the race, I have kept the faith" (2 Timothy 4:7). Paul's point seems to be that Timothy should be diligent in his work despite what happens in the world and in the churches around him. Paul's self-worth was not bound up in what others did or didn't do, did or didn't believe, or did or didn't feel.

Like Paul, if pastors are going to be able to call their congregations "beloved," they are going to have to distance themselves from them.[5] They will have to remember that their calling and approval come from God, not man. And sometimes God calls us to fields that, to human eyes, don't yield much in the way of a harvest. God, however, will go to extravagant lengths just to save one individual (Matthew 18:12–14; Acts 8:26–39). Could it be that God brought you to your current church so that your talents and gifts could be used to touch, save, and nurture just those few souls there? Even if you don't see any people converted or growing more mature in the Lord, it doesn't necessarily mean that God is displeased with your ministry. Maybe, like Isaiah, yours is meant to be the voice of judgment, not renewal (Isaiah 6:9–10). Perhaps your people aren't blocking what God has in mind for you to do after all.

And they can't block what you have in mind for yourself. There are ways to advance your career while serving a small church that don't depend upon the small church. You can get involved in doing work for your denomination, your local fellowship of churches, or a parachurch organization.[6] Let those outside your small church get to know you and notice your gifts, so that whatever your congregation does or doesn't decide to do, you'll have references who appreciate what you are capable of. More importantly, such work will remind you that God's kingdom is much bigger than the four walls of little Faith Fellowship Church, show you that there will always be a place for you in that kingdom, and allow you to minister using gifts and abilities you aren't called on to use much in that small church.

It's crucial that your world becomes and remains bigger than your small church. You must take at least one day totally off, away from church work and church people. Start a hobby or two. Do some reading that isn't related to your job. Rent some old movies on video. Take a walk. Learn to golf or bowl. Have a picnic in a park that is three towns over from your church. Whatever you do with your time off, make sure it is really "down time" and you fight even the thoughts about the congregation that flit through your mind during that time.

If all this sounds "unspiritual," ask yourself why God commanded us to keep the Sabbath day holy. What does it mean for a pastor to "cease from his (or her) labor"? Remember that no less a spiritual giant than Martin Luther prescribed working in the garden or going to a dance as an antidote to spiritual depression.[7] A vacation can often have the same effect as a revival! A vacation will help you view your congregation with fresh, and often more appreciative, eyes. Chances are, while you are away ministry will still go on—services will be held, friends will counsel and encourage one another, the youth group will have a bottle drive, etc. You'll start to realize that God's work in your church doesn't depend on you alone. This, in turn, will make you more comfortable with the idea of taking time off, more willing to delegate responsibility, and more receptive to the ideas of your people.

Purposely distancing yourself from your church by remembering that your calling and approval come from God and not man, getting involved with the larger church, and taking time off may seem, at first glance, to insure that you will end up caring less rather than more for your people. Just the opposite is true, however. You will begin to be able to love more because the fear factor will be shrinking. It works for Pastor Adam.

Adam is the epitome of the "caring pastor." He counts it a privilege to sit with an elderly woman in a hospital waiting room for three hours while her husband undergoes surgery. If called to mediate a marital dispute at 11:00 P.M., he will go and stay until midnight or 3:00 A.M., if necessary, counseling the couple and reminding them of the power of Christ. Pastor Adam has been known to spend hours on his knees in his office agonizing with God over the sins and problems he sees in his church. His congregation is not perfect. They've had their share of power struggles, personality clashes, misunderstandings, and hard financial times. But Pastor Adam would agree with Al LaValley who says that in a church, "People get upset and angry from time to time at each other just like in a family: however, a marriage isn't dissolved at one fight."[8] Pastor Adam's "marriage" with his congregation has lasted over fifteen years, and he has no plans to leave. He appreciates the fact that he ministers among people he knows. He isn't performing marriages for strangers but for friends. When he mourns, he mourns with family members. He also values the many lessons in faith, perseverance, and Christian living that his congregation has taught him. He recalls with affection the members who have supported him when he and his family went through tough times.

But one of the main secrets of Pastor Adam's longevity is the advice he gives to young pastors: "Love your people, but don't trust yourself to them." By this, he doesn't mean that you aren't to be open and honest with others in general but rather that you must practice distancing yourself from your congregation and drawing close to God. As involved with his people as he is, Pastor Adam still does not let his life become totally bound up in them. Barring emergencies, he takes one full day off a week and during the week, when he has a spare hour or two, he takes his wife to lunch, shoots baskets with his son, or browses in old bookstores. He sees to it that he spends time studying the Scriptures. He also reads stimulating Christian books for himself. He does not do these things just to help him prepare sermons. Rather, he wants to make sure that the loudest, clearest voice he hears is the voice of the Lord and not the vice president of the board. Pastor Adam is actively involved in helping his denomination start new churches in his area. He often takes the church planters under his wing, offering them empathy, support, and direction.

Because Pastor Adam is able to separate himself from his church, he does not fear them. Instead, he is able to treasure his congregation for who they are and see God working corporately and individually in the lives of the members. In his words they are, "the joy of his life."

The aim of this book has been to help you to see that ministry in the small church can be a true joy. Hopefully, you have gained some insight into the nature of small congregations and have realized that they are not evil—just different. I trust that you have picked up some pointers which will enable you to wisely lead a small church forward for Christ. And my desire is that you, like Pastor Adam, can come to cherish your people and to echo the words of the following song, which speaks about the love within a small church or fellowship group.

Those Who Walk Beside

by Deborah J. Bierly[9]

Thank the Lord for those who walk beside,
on the way to his land,
For how could we ever reach the place,
without their loving hands?

(Chorus)
Thank the Lord, thank the Lord,
and be grateful for his care
that he shows us in the arms of those
whose lives we have come to share. (repeat chorus)

Reaching out to love and comfort us
when all the world seems cold,
Standing with us in our darkest hour,
Always there as we grow old.

Learn to love the ones He's given you,
Bear with them and forgive,
Speak the truth in love with gentleness,
For they put their trust in Him.

Appendix 1:
Questions Answered

Question #1: *How can you compare pastoring a small church with being a missionary? America is one of the most Christianized nations in the world. A pastor is not breaking new ground for the Gospel. He or she is going to an already established church in order to minister to a Christian congregation. Pastors are preaching to the converted: people who should know better than to put up with the heel-dragging, infighting, and fear of change that are present in so many small churches.*

Answer #1: In claiming that pastors should adopt a missionary mindset, I'm not necessarily claiming that small-church pastors are breaking new ground for the Gospel. Pastors and missionaries are alike in that they both need to learn how to minister in cultures that are alien to them.

If, however, I was claiming that pastors in small churches were breaking new ground for the Gospel, would I be so wrong? The vast majority of people in North America—about nineteen out of twenty in the United States—may say that they believe in God, but how much difference does that belief make in their lives?[1] Aren't Americans very much like the Athenians in Acts 17, "extremely religious" (v. 22), yet without a clue about who the true God really is? American pastors seem to think so. In regular conversations, many pastors state that their main job is to try to convert the church.

People join small congregations for reasons other than commitment to Christ. Some attend a small church because, "This is where my grandfather worshiped all his life." Some choose a small church because they want to be big fish in a small pond. Others are seeking attention and support as they struggle with their problems. Still others join because it's the traditional thing to do when one is establishing a home in the community. A pastor ought not to assume that his or her congregation is converted just because the sign out front says First Christian Church.

Question #2: *You advocate being content with small steps and caution that progress in the small church takes a long time. Where is the sense of the urgency of the Gospel in your style of ministry?*

Answer #2: I have read books and articles on the small church which seem to advocate that the only thing a pastor should intentionally work toward is becoming one of the congregation.

This is not, however, what leadership is all about. A leader should intentionally set out to bring growth, change, unity, vision, and excellence to his or her congregation. My point is that the small-church culture will only allow these things to happen over time. Certainly, a leader should work just as fast as a congregation will let him or her go.

One doesn't give up urgency or intentionality when one accepts a call to a small church. One works intentionally and urgently to the best of his or her ability to find ways to operate within the small-church system to bring about needed change. Those who try to work against or outside of the system soon find themselves without a call.

Question #3: *There doesn't seem to be much "boldly speaking the truth in love" in the style of ministry you present. When problems arise in the church, why shouldn't we just confront them head-on? When situations need correcting, why not just step in and correct them?*

Answer #3: Different relationships, different situations, and different congregations call for different responses from the Christian leader. The New Testament gives Paul as a case in point. The same apostle Paul who got tough with heresy and gross immorality in some churches (Galatians 3:1; 1 Corinthians 5:3–5), took a more backdoor relational approach when dealing with Philemon (see especially Philemon 8–9). Paul urged (not commanded) Euodia and Syntyche to reach agreements in Christ and asked the rest of the congregation to help them work through their problems (Philippians 4:2–3). Paul also gave up his apostolic right to be financially supported by the church because he felt it would be an obstacle to the Corinthians' acceptance of the Gospel. He claimed that he tried to be all things to all people in order to save some (1 Corinthians 9). Once when Paul was discussing such important doctrinal points as leaving behind claims of personal righteousness in order to know Christ, attaining the resurrection from the dead, and making progress in sanctification, he said, in effect, "If anyone disagrees with me about any of this, don't sweat it. God will show you the truth in time" (Philippians 3:15). It's obvious that Paul constantly adapted his ministry style to fit his audience.

Is there anything wrong, then, with deciding that dealing with small churches calls for the style of ministry described in this book? This style of ministry isn't unbiblical. Indeed, it is in line with what the Wisdom Literature teaches us about respecting human powers that be, cultivating friendships, and watching the tongue.

There will certainly be times when the leader of the small church must draw the line and get tough. Before one decides to take a stand, however, one should pray for discernment. Seeking the counsel of others is also advisable. Often the issue a leader wants to go to the mat for is not worth the risk of potentially ending his or her ministry in the congregation. In many cases there are alternative ways to handle a problem which will bring resolution and honor to Christ, without "bloody" confrontations. I'm interested in exploring those alternatives.

Appendix 1

Question #4: *You seem to be overly optimistic about small churches. Obviously, you've never met my congregation. They are driving me nuts!! Are you saying that I've got to hang in there with them forever? Isn't it biblical to shake the dust off one's feet and move on?*

Answer #4: There are churches that suck the vitality and joy right out of their leaders (Hebrews 13:17). Other congregations are about to have their lampstands removed by the Lord because of heresy, sloth, or disobedience (Revelation 2 and 3). Some small churches can't or won't give their pastors decent salaries (1 Corinthians 9:7–14; 1 Timothy 5;17–18).

If you are serving in one of the above congregations, maybe the best advice anyone could give you is to move on. However, why not move with a clear conscience, knowing that you've done everything you could to change the church? Why not first try ministering in the style presented in this book? There are no magic guarantees for those who do, but often leaders will be surprised at how a stubborn church begins to come around once leaders start adapting to the small church's culture.

For more help with evaluating your congregation and determining whether to stay or go, I recommend these books:

Haugh, Kenneth. *Antagonists in the Church.* Minneapolis: Augsburg Press, 1988.

Merrill, Dean. *Clergy Couples in Crisis.* Waco: Christianity Today and Word Books, 1985.

Robbins, Paul D., ed., *When It's Time to Move.* Waco: Christianity Today and Word Books, 1985.

Wagner, C. Peter. *Your Church Can Be Healthy.* Nashville: Abingdon Press, 1979.

Appendix 2:
Recommended Reading and Words of Caution

The best books I've found relating to small-church ministry:

Hughes, Kent and Barbara. *Liberating Ministry from the Success Syndrome.* Wheaton, IL: Tyndale House Publishers, 1987.

Oswald, Roy M. *New Beginnings: A Pastorate Start-Up Workbook.* New York: The Alban Institute, 1989.

Pappas, Anthony G. *Entering the World of the Small Church.* New York: The Alban Institute, 1988.

Pappas, Anthony G. *Money, Motivation, and Mission in the Small Church.* Valley Forge, PA: Judson Press, 1989.

Patterson, Ben. *Waiting.* Downers Grove, IL: InterVarsity Press, 1989.

Peterson, Eugene H. *The Contemplative Pastor.* Waco: Christianity Today and Word Books, 1989.

Peterson, Eugene H. *Under the Unpredictable Plant.* Grand Rapids: William B. Eerdmans Publishing Company, 1992.

Schaller, Lyle E. *The Small Church Is Different.* Nashville: Abingdon Press, 1982.

Senter, Ruth. *So You're the Pastor's Wife.* Grand Rapids: Zondervan Publishing House, 1979.

Shelley, Marshall. *Well-Intentioned Dragons.* Waco: Christianity Today and Word Books, 1985.

Willimon, William H. and Wilson, Robert L. *Preaching and Worship in the Small Church.* Nashville: Abingdon Press, 1980.

Appendix 2
Caution: Dangerous When Read

When you read books on how to be a church leader, beware of unfavorably comparing yourself to authors who are church planters or pastors of larger congregations. Church planters are often able to make gains quickly because they are the tribal leaders of their groups. They don't have to win over key figures and founding families to their ways of thinking. They are the key figures and founding families. And pastors of larger churches minister in a different environment than you do. Large churches tend to be goal-oriented, not tradition-bound. The large church spends their time figuring out ways to move forward. The small church spends their time making sure existing members are kept happy. The large church has unlimited resources. The small church may not be able to pay the pastor this year, and they still haven't found anyone to teach the junior high Sunday school class.

Your reading should be challenging, but not disheartening. Read too many books by "successful" pastors serving in other fields of ministry and you will begin to believe that the movement of God has passed you by. Nothing could be further from the truth. Remember that the Good Shepherd who searches for one lost sheep (Luke 15:3–7) and who loved the church at Smyrna (Revelation 2:8–11) won't turn his back on the small church. Choose books that help you see God in your ministry, not books that imply he's doing his best work elsewhere.

Don't limit your reading to books on how to make it in the small church. You need to keep a big picture of God and of the church of Jesus Christ as you labor in your congregation. Books on theology, biblical studies, church history, world missions, etc. will give you such a picture. Don't become provincial in your thinking, focusing solely on the concerns of the local church. Don't let your small congregation set the boundaries of your world (or God's world, for that matter).

Appendix 3:
The Cobblestone Commission

The following is a three-year outreach plan that was approved by the governing board (the consistory) of the small congregation I serve—the Second Reformed Church of Rotterdam, a.k.a. Cobblestone Church, or just plain Cobblestone.

The document is included to give the reader another example of how the ideas presented in this book look when they are "fleshed out."

Notice that while the plan isn't as ambitious as some plans that come out of the church-growth movement, it does move the church forward while allowing the congregation to retain their identity. It is progressive, yet nonthreatening.

In drafting the plan, I deliberately refrained from saying, "As your pastor, here's what I believe we need to do." Instead, I assumed the role of a servant, helping the congregation accomplish what they wanted to see happen. The plan provides for congregational input throughout the three years, and I made it clear that I based my conclusions of what Cobblestone is like on direct input from the members of the church. I wanted the church to feel that this was their plan and not just "some crazy idea from the pastor."

The Cobblestone Commission

A Three-Year Outreach Plan

January 1993–December 1995

I. Introduction

Appendix 3

In the church profile that was sent to me when I was candidating, the search committee indicated that evangelism was one of the church's top priorities. In an attachment explaining their choice, they wrote:

"We feel this means *you* preparing *us* to impact our community for the Lord." (emphasis theirs)

When I read this, I became very excited because it showed me that the search committee was in tune with the Lord. In Matthew 28:18–20, Jesus gave these "marching orders" to the church:

Then Jesus came to them and said, "All authority in heaven and on earth has been given to me. Therefore go and make disciples of all nations, baptizing them in the name of the Father and of the Son and of the Holy Spirit, and teaching them to obey everything I have commanded you. And surely I am with you always, to the very end of the age."

II. Cobblestone's Identity and the Implications

From the dinners my wife and I hosted where you were encouraged to share your thoughts about the church, and from private conversations and planning meetings for various church programs and committees, I have come to the conclusion that most people attend Cobblestone for one or more of the following reasons:

1. Family and friends either attend here or have attended at some time in the past.
2. The congregation is very open and friendly.
3. It's a small church, so members can get to know one another and develop close relationships.
4. The church provides a support group—it's one big family.
5. The building is located close to where most members live.
6. It's a Bible-believing and teaching church.

7. There's a good age mix in the church with no one age group predominating.

I see no reason to assume that God wants us to be something radically different from what we are because he has brought the church to where we are today. I believe that God wants us to be ourselves, just as long as we are becoming the best "ourselves" that we can possibly be. With this in mind, it seems to me that the people Cobblestone Church are most likely to reach are:

1. Friends, family members, and coworkers of church members.
2. People living within a two to three mile radius from the church.
3. Lonely, hurting people who are looking for support, friends, and a new (or larger) family.

I'm not saying that we won't reach people who aren't in one of the categories above, only that I believe these categories describe our primary mission field. It seems that God has called us to be a small, local, warm, caring congregation, and that we will attract people who are looking for that kind of church. Therefore, our efforts in evangelism as a congregation should be primarily focused on people in these three categories. This means, for example, that we won't spend a lot of money on advertising, hoping to draw people from all over the capitol district. We don't need to be concerned with getting big-name speakers or singers to come and put on mega-events. We don't need to restructure our worship service to appeal primarily to baby boomers and yuppies, or to senior citizens. In short, all of our evangelistic methods and ideas should be true to what God has made us.

With this in mind, let me propose the following three-year plan. At any time it may be modified by the consistory. The spiritual life and fellowship committee would have the primary

Appendix 3

responsibility for seeing that the plan is carried out. I would like to serve as chairperson of this committee. The plan consists of three main elements:

A. Seeking the Lord
B. Sowing the Seed
C. Sealing the Commitment

A. Seeking the Lord

If the Lord isn't guiding, supporting, and working through our evangelistic efforts, we'll be wasting our time (Psalm 127:1; Colossians 4:3; 1 Corinthians 2:14).

1. Every time a group in the church assembles for a spiritual purpose, prayer would be offered for the lost (we wouldn't have to do this at a picnic or game night). This means that at every meeting/rehearsal for three years the Sunday school classes, committees, consistory, Triple P fellowship, youth groups, women's fellowship, VBS teachers, the choir, etc. would offer at least a short prayer for the unreached and for power and wisdom to reach them. (If needed, I can provide written prayers to use for the first several months until everyone is comfortable with the process.)

2. Once a quarter, the church would be open all day until early evening for people to come and pray for specific unsaved friends and relatives and for those living within a two- to three-mile radius of the church. People could also spend time thanking God for the blessings they have received from his hand working through Cobblestone Church and ask him to bless others as well through this ministry.

3. I would keep myself and others informed about the evangelistic methods, programs, and insights the Lord has been blessing elsewhere. This is an interest of mine and I will gladly keep reading books and articles, listening to tapes, watching videos, and attending workshops on the subject of church growth. If anyone feels the Lord is calling them to work with me on this, I

would love to take them to seminars or watch videos or share and discuss materials with them. I will also pass along ideas and resources to the committee for discussion.

4. We would continue to ask for and look at other ideas relating to seeking the Lord from the committee, consistory, and congregation.

B. Sowing the Seed

We need to take the message of the Gospel to those outside of Cobblestone (Matthew 13:1–23; Luke 15:1–32; Revelation 12:10–11).

1. Once a year, I would teach a workshop on an aspect of witnessing. These workshops would probably follow a Friday-night-through-Saturday format. They could be video or audio taped for those unable to attend. The workshops would be:

1993: "Friendship Evangelism"

1994: "How to Give a Clear Presentation of the Gospel to Practically Anybody"

1995: "How to Witness to Those Who Already Know It All"

2. At least twice a year, we would put on a special event at the church ("Friend Day," talent/concert night, video night, etc.). Members can invite friends and family to these events knowing that they will hear the Gospel in a low pressure, nonthreatening way.

3. We would either find and purchase, or write and have printed, good witnessing tools that our congregation can use. We would have these available for anyone to take.

4. We would ask for and look at other ideas relating to sowing the seed from the committee, consistory, and congregation.

C. Sealing the Commitment

If you look closely again at Matthew 28:18–20, you'll notice that the church's task is to make disciples. We're not just to invite a person to visit the church once, or just to pray for him or her

Appendix 3

to receive Christ (as important as this is), but we are also to encourage that person to join a fellowship of Christians where he or she can grow in the knowledge, power, and love of the Lord.

1. We must find an effective way to greet, meet, and follow-up on visitors.

2. We need to be alert for and correct areas of "sociological strangulation" that may be impeding growth. "Sociological strangulation" is a technical term for "the inability of the physical facilities to keep up with the people flow" (C. Peter Wagner, "How to Break the 200 Barrier," a seminar sponsored by the Charles E. Fuller Institute of Evangelism and Church Growth).

For example:

The sanctuary becomes so full that visitors perceive there is no room for them.

The only seats available for visitors are "down front."

Visitors can't find a place to park.

Visitors have a small baby and the nursery isn't properly equipped or cleaned.

Visitors can't easily find bathrooms, the nursery, Sunday school rooms, etc.

If any of the above happens, there's a good chance a visitor won't come back a second time.

3. Two times a year (probably fall and spring), the six week class *Belonging* (Reformed Church Press) would be offered to existing members and potential members/inquirers during the Sunday school hour.

4. We would ask for and look at other ideas relating to sealing the commitment from the committee, consistory, and congregation.

III. Beyond 1995

During 1995, the committee would work closely with me in evaluating what Cobblestone has done for evangelism: what parts of the plan worked well and why; what parts didn't and why; and where God is calling us to go from here. The committee will submit a three-year plan for 1996–1998 to the consistory for approval at their October 1995 meeting.

Appendix 4:
The Cobblestone Mission Statement

Shortly before a regularly scheduled consistory (our church board) meeting, I gave our members the following to read:

I. The Need

1. When I first came to Cobblestone, my wife and I hosted dinners out of which grew "The Cobblestone Commission," the church's three-year outreach plan. I took what the congregation told me of their impressions of Cobblestone and dreams for the future, combined them with some of my own, and came up with a document everyone could endorse. Soon it will be time to put together another plan, and I'd like some fresh input in order to be able to do it.

2. Because we have tried many new things already, and because I'm still "the new minister," people are freely sharing their ideas with me. I've heard ideas about how fast and how much we should grow, the style of worship we should use, and new programs we should try. Unfortunately, two people in a row don't necessarily share the same ideas about these subjects. What is lacking is a unified vision of what Cobblestone is all about and where the church is heading.

3. People are letting me know they have certain gifts that they'd like to use in our church for the Lord. At present, however, we can't use all of them. I need to have a clear picture of where we are heading so I can tell people, "In the near future, we're going to need someone like you. Here's where you fit at Cobblestone."

Appendix 4

The church needs a brief (no longer than one page) but important mission statement to guide our ministry in the foreseeable future. Such a statement would look something like this:

Cobblestone Church is a: _____

_____

Congregation that emphasizes:_____

_____

For our members we provide: _____

_____

For the community we provide: _____

_____

When we worship together we: _____

_____

Here are some examples of how such a statement would be used to guide ministry:

a. If our statement says we are a friendly church who emphasizes warmth and caring, then the only evangelistic strategies we would consider are those that help the church to grow while allowing members to have close ties with others in the congregation.

b. If our statement says we are open to new ways of worshiping the Lord, then we would encourage more lay participation in worship, more contemporary congregational singing, drama, etc.

c. If our statement says we provide our members with a place to belong, then we would make being in contact with everyone (especially new members) one of our top priorities, to make sure they really "feel at home," their opinions are heard, and their gifts are used.

d. If our statement says we emphasize evangelism and desire to grow as much as possible, then, in addition to increasing outreach, we would work on the overcrowding problem in the sanctuary, train more lay visitation ministers and more teachers, etc.

II. Possible Ways to Create Such a Statement

1. As pastor I could draft a statement, and the consistory could adopt it as their own. I'm willing to do this, if you so desire. I do have dreams for our future. However, I know that I'm not the only one with insight and that God can and does speak through you too. Cobblestone is YOUR church. The vision must be yours as well as mine.

2. A subcommittee of the consistory could work with me on such a statement. But, honestly, don't you sometimes feel committeed and meetinged to death?

3. The consistory could take a retreat in order to put some concentrated effort into drafting such a statement. This could be overnight at a retreat center. It could also be right at Cobblestone or at another church in the area (provided we could not be interrupted except for REAL EMERGENCIES; not have members running off to do errands, transport the family, etc.; not feel rushed for time; and have "breaks," which are very important if one is to continue doing profitable work).

The retreat option is the one I prefer; however, I am open to the others.

III. A Format for a Retreat

We would first share our responses to questions on worksheets you'd receive in advance. There wouldn't be any surprise questions or topics brought up at the retreat. We would come to a consensus on what the mission statement should say and then agree to operate according to the statement either for the foreseeable future or a set number of years. We would be in prayer for the retreat before it happens and enlist the congregation to pray as well.

The questions would have no "right" or "wrong" answers but would be designed to let us know, honestly, how others feel.

They would be discussion starters. We would need to come to the retreat seeking the Lord, seeking understanding, seeking direction, and seeking consensus. We should not come seeking to "convert the consistory to my way of thinking," or asserting that things have got to be "my way or I hit the highway."[1]

———

I then gave the consistory some sample questions and proposed several different schedules for a retreat. At the meeting, the consistory decided to have a retreat right at Cobblestone. With members' work schedules and family commitments, it seemed to be the only way we could ensure good attendance. The Friday night/Saturday morning schedule we finally agreed on was:

SCHEDULE:

FRIDAY P.M.

     5:30: Devotional on the body of Christ
     5:45: First work session
     6:15: Supper (potluck, catered, or delivered)
     7:00: Worship and the Lord's Supper[2]
     7:30: Second work session
     8:30: Break
     8:45: Third work session
     9:30: Home

SATURDAY A.M.

     8:30: Devotional on the body of Christ
     8:45: Fourth work session
     9:45: Break (coffee and donuts)
   10:00: Fifth work session
   11:00: Break (fruit)
   11:15: Sixth work session, if needed
   12:15: Home

The following is the questionnaire I handed out to the consistory before the retreat. The members were asked to fill it out as honestly as they could and come prepared to share their answers.

1. What three to five adjectives or descriptive phrases would you use to tell a friend about Cobblestone?

2. Are there any words or phrases you *wish* you could use to describe Cobblestone, but in all honesty can't?

3. When I dream of what Cobblestone will be like ten years from now, I see it as (check all that apply):

    _____   much the same as it is now.
    _____   having a full sanctuary.
    _____   about the size of Princetown or Bellevue Reformed.
    _____   having multiple, multiflavored worship services and programs.
    _____   having multiple staff (ex. youth pastor, visitation pastor, etc.).
    _____   quietly meeting the needs of the people God brings us.
    _____   a small, neighborhood church.
    _____   a model church and a trendsetter that other churches can learn from.
    _____   other _____
    _____   _____
    _____   _____

My dream makes me feel (check all that apply):
    _____   sad.
    _____   very much at home.
    _____   displaced.

Appendix 4

_____ contented.

_____ great.

_____ challenged.

_____ confused because I don't know how we're going to get there.

_____ confident because God will take us there.

_____ frustrated because this group will never get there.

4. Given that all healthy churches grow in four areas, rank the areas (1–4) in order of importance to you:

   _____ Growing up (Acts 2:42).

   _____ Growing together (Acts 2:44).

   _____ Growing out—the early church gained a good reputation in the community (Acts 2:47).

   _____ Growing in numbers (Acts 2:47).[3]

5. When it comes to numerical growth, I believe (check all that apply):

   _____ we're too concerned about it.

   _____ if we continue to preach and teach the Word of God and be who we are, the Lord will automatically add to our numbers.

   _____ it's okay as long as it doesn't disrupt the "family feeling" Cobblestone has.

   _____ it's okay as long as it doesn't upset any of our long-term members.

   _____ we need to plan for it—after all, you hit what you aim for.

   _____ we need to do more in the area of evangelism.

   _____ we should do everything in our power (even making radical changes) to help Cobblestone grow.

   _____ it's essential for Cobblestone's future survival.

   _____ other _____

_____   _____

_____   _____

6. Below is a list of some of the programs, services, and activities Cobblestone offers. On the line before each activity, rate it according to how important you feel it is for Cobblestone. Use this key:

E—Essential. Must keep program going at all costs.

V—Very Important. This or something like it plays a major role in determining a church's vitality. One of the last things I'd drop.

I—Important. Adds to church's growth and health. We should try to keep this or something like it going, but if staff, money, and interest aren't there, we could drop it.

N—Not very important. Not a high priority to keep it going.

D—Drop it tomorrow as far as I'm concerned.

_____   Adult Sunday School

_____   Adult Bible Studies

_____   Youth Fellowship

_____   Jesus Machine

_____   Vacation Bible School

_____   Children's Sunday School

_____   Women's Fellowship Breakfast

_____   Men's Fellowship Breakfast

_____   Social Events (talent show, Mexican night, picnic, etc.)

_____   Day of Prayer

_____   Prayer Chain

_____   Learning Dinners

_____   Family dinners after church to teach about aspects of worship and the sacraments

_____   Evangelism Seminars

_____   Semiannual Men's or Women's Banquets

Appendix 4

_____ Teaching Tapes
_____ Book Cart and Library

7. I want my church to help me (choose up to four):

_____ be aware of the needs of others in Rotterdam and the surrounding area.

_____ be aware of the needs of others in the congregation.

_____ be aware of the needs of other churches in the area.

_____ build good moral foundations for my personal life.

_____ see that life is worth living and has meaning.

_____ share my faith with others.

_____ teach my children about God and help me raise them properly.

_____ solve my personal problems.

_____ mature in the Christian faith.

_____ understand the Bible.

_____ develop a circle of close friends.

_____ find ways to spend my leisure time that are fun, relaxing, and pleasing to God.

_____ serve God in the realms of politics and local government.

_____ work for justice in my community and in my world.

I believe that my desires (check any that apply):

_____ match those of the majority of people at Cobblestone.

_____ match those of some of the people at Cobblestone.

_____ may reflect the mind of the congregation.

_____ may not reflect the mind of the congregation.

_____ probably don't reflect the mind of the congregation.

_____ are mine alone.

8. In relation to other churches and Christian organizations in the area, Cobblestone should be (check all that apply):

_____ kept aware of what's happening in the capitol district.

_____ cooperating at about the level we are now.

_____ aggressively participate (through prayer, finances, and labor) in everything we possibly can.

_____ cautious that we don't overextend ourselves.

_____ interested, but we should realize that ministry in the local church comes first.

9. What are some words and phrases you would use to describe the worship service at Cobblestone?

10. What are some words and phrases you *wish* you could use to describe the worship service at Cobblestone, but in all honesty can't?

11. In worship services it is important to (check any you believe):

_____ follow a set, standard format, except for rare occasions.

_____ experiment with new formats and ways of helping the congregation experience God.

_____ make everyone feel at home.

_____ teach people new songs.

_____ reflect our history and tradition.

_____ follow the Spirit's leading.

_____ always have a sermon.

_____ present the Word of God in new ways (i.e., drama, dance, videos).

_____ make sure we sing at least one "golden oldie" hymn.

_____ hold it on Sunday mornings.

_____ reflect the liturgical calendar.

12. If it were up to me, I'd make sure the worship service (check all that apply):

_____ stayed much the same as it is now.

_____ included more praise/worship songs and choruses more often.

_____ had more lay participation.

_____ had fewer announcements.

_____ had more music.

_____ had more special speakers and outside groups.

_____ included manifestations of the "miraculous" spiritual gifts.

_____ other _____

_____ _____

_____ _____

I believe that my desires expressed in questions 11 and 12 (check any that apply):

_____ match those of the majority of people at Cobblestone.

_____ match those of some of the people at Cobblestone.

_____ may reflect the mind of the congregation.

_____ may not reflect the mind of the congregation.

_____ probably don't reflect the mind of the congregation.

_____ are mine alone.

The congregation was informed about the upcoming retreat through our church's newsletter, the Sunday morning announcements, and word of mouth. Church members were urged to do two things to help the retreat be successful—pray for it and make sure the consistory would be uninterrupted when they met together. They gladly complied, and more than one consistory member came to the retreat anticipating good things to happen because people were praying.

Good things happened indeed. I went right around the room asking members to share their responses to the questions. I recorded these responses on a pad of newsprint. When we felt we had heard enough answers to be able to fill in some of the blanks in our mission statement, we did so. For example, questions 1 and 2 helped us fill in "Cobblestone Church is a congregation. . . ." Questions 3 through 7 helped spell out for us what we wanted to emphasize in our ministry and what sorts of things we wanted to provide for our members. At our final work session, we edited the statement into its final form.

Here is the statement we wrote:

Cobblestone Church Mission Statement

- Cobblestone is a Bible-believing church of warm, friendly, caring people, who emphasize spiritual growth and fellowship.
- We provide educational and social opportunities for both adults and children in our congregation.
- We are an extended family in the Lord, seeking to meet one another's needs.
- We are a Christian family, worshiping the Lord together in the RCA tradition. We value the preaching and teaching of the Word of God, praising the Lord through music, and sharing one another's joys and struggles. We also provide for special worship opportunities in a variety of formats.

- Through friendship evangelism we seek to introduce other people to Christ, reaching out to the community through vacation Bible school, youth ministry, informal social events, concerts, seminars, community action, counseling, and worship opportunities.

The consistory adopted the statement as their guidelines for ministry for the foreseeable future and published it in our church's newsletter. They also decided to print it in the front of our directory and our committee bylaws. Twice a year the statement would be read at regularly scheduled consistory meetings, and we would discuss how well we felt we were living up to it.

Apart from allowing us to draft the statement, the retreat was valuable in bringing the consistory together in Christian fellowship. Many members expressed a desire to have one the following year. The joys of accomplishing a difficult task and working through to a consensus on our future did not quickly fade away.

Please Note Well:

1. As with the Cobblestone Commission (see Appendix 3), I based the need for a mission statement in the congregation's desires, questions, and concerns. I did not declare to my people, "Any church who wants to grow needs to have a clear vision. We need to have a retreat in order to come up with a mission statement."
2. I included the consistory in the process of planning the retreat.
3. I let the church define itself. I didn't tell it what it ought to be. My job now is to help the congregation live up to their stated identity, not to try and make them into something they aren't.[4]

Notes

Introduction

1. Lyle E. Schaller, *The Small Church Is Different* (Nashville: Abingdon Press, 1982), p. 180.

Chapter One: But I Followed the Instructions!

1. Roy M. Oswald, *New Beginnings* (New York: The Alban Institute, 1989), p. 43.
2. Schaller, p. 144.
3. Quoted by Dean Merrill, *Clergy Couples in Crisis* (Waco: Christianity Today and Word Books, 1985), p. 15.
4. By the small church's "culture," I mean "the values and behavior that are expected among members of a particular social group. The culture is an unspoken set of assumptions and actions—the way we do it around here." Carl S. Dudley and Douglas Alan Walrath, *Developing Your Small Church's Potential* (Valley Forge, PA: Judson Press, 1988), p. 51.

Chapter Two: Out of the Ivory Palaces

1. Marshall Shelley, *Well-Intentioned Dragons* (Waco: Word Publishing and Christianity Today, 1985), p. 13.
2. Large-church pastors can be considered to come from the business world as they often manage their churches the way CEOs manage their companies.
3. By "business world" I'm not referring exclusively to corporate America. A family farm is a small business. I'm referring to vocations where there's an excellent chance that hard work (i.e., long hours, careful planning, keeping up on the latest techniques, etc.) will equal success.

4. For an on-target discussion of American culture and its effect on the church, see David F. Wells, *No Place for Truth or Whatever Happened to Evangelical Theology?* (Grand Rapids: Eerdmans, 1993).

5. Speakers at a Charles E. Fuller Institute of Evangelism and Church Growth seminar, "Breaking the 200 Barrier," stressed that pastors are not in the "church," "theology," or "religion," business. Instead, they are in the "people" business.

Chapter Three: Family Resemblances

1. Bill M. Sullivan, *Ten Steps to Breaking the 200 Barrier* (Kansas City: Beacon Hill Press, 1988), p. 13.

2. Anthony G. Pappas, *Entering the World of the Small Church* (New York: The Alban Institute, 1988), pp. 9–15.

3. Schaller, p. 144.

4. Pappas, pp. 9, 21.

5. John C. Maxwell's discussion on "Breaking the 200 Barrier." Copyright 1992 by Maxwell. Sponsored by the Charles E. Fuller Institute of Evangelism and Church Growth. Held in Pittsburg, PA, 1992.

6. C. Peter Wagner, *Leading Your Church to Grow* (Venture, CA: Regal Books, 1984), p. 103.

7. Oswald, p. 29.

Chapter Four: One of the Gang

1. Acting comes more naturally to some personalities and temperaments than others. Also, some can fit right into the life of a small congregation without doing any acting at all. There is a sense in which small-church leaders are born, not made. Before you conclude that you are a square peg in a round hole, however, try doing some acting and see what happens. You might be pleasantly surprised.

2. Conflict is inevitable. However, it is not a sure sign that you should change churches, schools, jobs, or spouses. Conflict was present in the early church (Acts 6:1; 15:1–2, 36–40; Philippians 4:2), and it will be present in our congregations,

too. As Eugene Peterson says, "Wherever two or three are gathered together, problems develop" (*The Contemplative Pastor*, Waco: Christianity Today and Word Books, 1989, p. 72). So we had better learn how to deal with conflicts.

Chapter Five: Let It Be

1. Pappas, p. 23.
2. To see how one congregation's outreach plan grew out of dinners like this, read Appendix 3: The Cobblestone Commission.
3. The wise pastoral candidate's response when a search committee maintains that they are tired of the status quo in their church is, "Well then, what are you doing about it? What are you planning to do about it in the immediate future?"

Chapter Six: Looking for God in All the Wrong Places

1. William H. Willimon and Robert L. Wilson, *Preaching and Worship in the Small Church* (Nashville: Abingdon Press, 1980), p. 42.
2. Anthony G. Pappas, *Money, Motivation, and Mission in the Small Church* (Valley Forge, PA: Judson Press, 1989), p. 20.
3. A critique of the church growth and related movements can be found in Douglas D. Webster, *Selling Jesus* (Downers Grove, IL: InterVarsity Press, 1992).
4. *Ecumenical Creeds and Reformed Confessions* (Grand Rapids: CRC Publications, 1988), p. 35.
5. Ibid., p. 108.
6. Schaller, p. 45.

Chapter Seven: Show Them the Termites

1. Pappas, *Entering the World*, pp. 26–27.
2. The leader certainly should give thought as to how he or she would solve a given problem, but should wait until asked ("Well, what do you think about this, Pastor?") before sharing those thoughts with the group. Once shared, the leader must accept the fact that his or her ideas won't automatically carry

any more weight than anyone else's. The leader is not a dictator, a king, a CEO, or a pope. The leader is just "one of the gang."

3. Pappas, *Entering the World*, pp. 82–84. Hostetler's book is *Amish Society*, 3d Edition, (Baltimore: The Johns Hopkins University Press, 1980).

4. I certainly believe in church discipline, but it is only *one* biblical way of solving problems in the church, and only to be used as a last resort. The apostle Paul didn't run around putting all the people who were engaging in immorality, backbiting, and idol worship in the early church under discipline. He tried to teach them a better way. He modeled for them the better way. He urged them to find ways to get along. I've known far too many leaders who seem anxious to skip all that and get right to taking disciplinary action.

Chapter Eight: From No Growth to Pro-Growth

1. Pappas, *Entering the World*, p. 14.
2. Wagner, p. 17.
3. These are the characteristics listed and elaborated on in Chapter 3.
4. If you haven't yet read Appendix 3: The Cobblestone Commission, now would be a good time to do so.
5. The way in which the board of the church I serve came to a consensus on the identity and mission of our congregation is detailed in Appendix 4: The Cobblestone Mission Statement.
6. Nancy E. Clark, "Sizing Up the Small Church," *Reformed Review* Vol. 47, No. 2 (Winter 1993–94): 121.

Chapter Nine: The Gospel in a Word Is Love

1. I strongly suspect that many lay leaders in the small church talk the same way about their congregations. I've heard more than a few of them myself.
2. As a friend of mine says, "The hardest part about being a good Christian leader is simply being a good Christian."

3. John C. Maxwell, *Be a People Person* (Wheaton, IL: Victor Books, 1989), p. 6.

4. Some of the fear that pastors feel toward their congregations is simply fear of the unknown. Members in a small church know each other, but the pastor doesn't know them. The way to overcome this fear is by getting to know your congregation, not just as pastor to parishioners, but as friend to friend. Host an open house or throw a party. Invite people over for a night of board games. Go out to dinner with a group from the church. Enjoy your congregation and they will enjoy you.

5. Although I am primarily addressing pastors in this chapter, lay leaders, too, must follow my advice and make sure they "get a life" outside of the workings and concerns of the local small church.

6. Or maybe, like one pastor who shall remain nameless, do some writing.

7. As Roland H. Bainton says on page 285 in *Here I Stand* (Nashville: Abingdon Press, 1978), "In all this advice to flee the fray Luther was in a way prescribing faith as a cure for the lack of faith. To give up the argument is of itself an act of faith . . . an expression of confidence in the restorative power of God, who operates in the subconscious while man occupies himself with extraneous things."

8. Al LaValley, *Being Poured Out* (Columbus, GA: Brentwood Christian Press, 1986), p. 54.

9. Copyright 1994 by Deborah J. Bierly. Used by permission.

Appendix 1: Questions Answered

1. *Beginnings* (Reformed Church Press, 1992), p. 7.

Appendix 4: The Cobblestone Mission Statement

1. We finally adopted the following rules of conduct for the retreat: we wouldn't pick on or put down anyone's ideas; that consensus, not persuasion or winning arguments, was our goal; and we would be open to the possibility that God could be speaking through any member at any given time.

2. This was led by a beloved, godly "elder emeritus" and was a very special time that helped set a positive, expectant tone for the entire retreat.

3. Adapted from C. Peter Wagner's discussion on "Breaking the 200 Barrier," Pittsburg, PA, 1992. Sponsored by the Charles E. Fuller Institute of Evangelism and Church Growth.

4. If it turns out that a congregation's identity and goals are not things a given leader can honestly live and work with, the leader can seriously consider moving elsewhere without feeling guilty about it.